# The Church at Prayer

## FRANK HAWKINS

**BROADMAN PRESS**
Nashville, Tennessee

4223-15

ISBN: 0-8054-2315-X

Dewey Decimal Classification: 252
Subject Headings: PRAYER MEETINGS // SERMONS - COLLECTIONS
Library of Congress Catalog Card Number: 85-15143
Printed in the United States of America

Scripture quotations are from the Revised Standard Version
of the Bible, copyrighted 1946, 1952, © 1971, 1973.

**Library of Congress Cataloging-in-Publication Data**

Hawkins, Frank, 1935-
   The church at prayer.

   1. Prayer meetings. I. Title.
BV285.H34   1986     264'.1      85-15143
ISBN 0-8054-2315-X

## Dedication

To my wife, Pat,
and our four children,
Perri, Greg, Todd, and Brad

# Contents

# 1

# A Believing Community

## Goal

To strengthen the church as a believing community.

## Scripture

And Jesus answered them, "Have faith in God. Truly, I say to you, whoever says to this mountain, 'Be taken up and cast into the sea,' and does not doubt in his heart, but believes that what he says will come to pass, it will be done for him. Therefore, I tell you, whatever you ask in prayer, believe that you have received it, and it will be yours (Mark 11:22-24).

## The Church at Prayer

The worship leader could involve the church in a prayer period focused toward strengthening belief through prayer. Various areas of belief could be mentioned as prayer topics. They are:

1. *Interpersonal Trust.* This kind of belief is necessary in all kinds of human relationships (i.e., parenting, marriage, teenage peer groups, singles, professional associates, committee members, etc.). The Holy Spirit will lead us to strengthen these areas of human trust if we ask in prayer, believing.

2. *Self-Confidence.* This is an area of trust we often overlook. Yet, its lack can block meaningful interpersonal trust. Young people are seeking to build it. Adults often face self-doubt and need to believe in themselves again.

3. *Trust in God.* All relational trust needs an anchor in one's confidence in God. The church and its members can be strengthened by a renewed awareness that God is trustworthy in prayer and in all human relationships.

It seemed like an impossible task as we heard Gail say, "I'm going to be a minister." We were lowly freshmen at Furman University, a Baptist College in Greenville, South Carolina. The first day of classes for the year 1957-58 had just ended, and we were walking lazily across the campus toward Geer Hall, a dormitory for male students.

Gail's words caused us to reflect on the classes of the day which had been so new to us. I say new, and yet, they had been repetitious in one sense. Each professor was careful to make sure we were properly introduced. "Please stand and give us your name and hometown" was the request which came at the beginning of each class. When the last class of the day started, Captain Sherman, an ROTC professor, made the same request.

Then it happened! Someone could not say his name. The class roared with laughter. We thought someone had finally forgotten his name. Then he tried again; he still could not say his name. We didn't laugh anymore. Gail Moul had a speech impediment. We felt so ashamed of ourselves.

When the class was over, we gathered around Gail and apologized. He forgave us with a smile as he said, "It's OK; you didn't know." As we walked across the campus, Gail told us about himself.

On December 7, 1941 he and his family were living at Pearl Harbor in the South Pacific. Gail's father was an officer in the United States Navy and had taken his family to the islands to be with him. That particular morning, Gail had gotten up early. He was looking out a window when the historic bombing of Pearl Harbor began. He saw the Japanese planes descend from the clouds. He heard a noise like thunder; and then, suddenly it came so near. A bomb exploded in a field close to their house. Gail was looking directly at the area where the bomb hit. According to Gail, something in him snapped which left him speechless.

After the planes left, Gail tried to talk; he couldn't. Days and weeks passed and he still could not communicate clearly. Thoughts were there in his keen mind, but his speech mechanism had been damaged by the exploding bomb.

Gail's parents took him to doctors at Pearl Harbor. When they returned to the United States, they took him to various specialists and received the same report from them all, "Your son has a permanent speech impediment."

We listened quietly as Gail struggled to share with us his story. When he finished, someone asked, "Gail, why did you come to Furman? What are you going to study here?" Without hesitation Gail said, "God has called me to be a minister; that's why I came to Furman." We didn't say anything; we didn't know what to say. That day, however, in the fall of 1957, that group of college freshmen became a believing community. We didn't know how Gail would be able to be a minister with this speech impediment. What mattered to us was that Gail believed it. That was enough for us. We accepted him and encouraged him, and, at the same time, received the acceptance and care which he gave to us.

Being a part of that believing community taught me something about the nature of faith. I learned that mountains can be moved by believing people. Jesus put it this way, "For truly, I say to you, if you have faith as a grain of mustard seed, you will say to this mountain, 'Move from here to there,' and it will move; and nothing will be impossible to you" (Matt. 17:20). Gail had a mountain which he was trying to move from his life. In varying degrees, every human being faces the challenge of moving mountains. At times a mountain may be a physical impediment with which one is born. A mountain may be acquired accidentally as a part of living. The mountains can be emotional and spiritual in nature; they expand upward as mountains of fear, doubt, anxiety, guilt, shame, hopelessness, and depression. Such mountains of the body, mind, and spirit may become so massive that lives are defeated and paralyzed.

Into these valleys of defeat there come the possibilities of belief. First, there comes God's belief in us. We cannot begin with our belief as being sufficient in the mountain-moving process. Our belief is possible because of God's belief in us. The coming of Christ to the world of persons speaks of God's power to believe people into a believing community. This truth of the Bible needs to be rediscovered and proclaimed to persons and church fellowships. Our capacity to believe dies if we stop believing in God's belief in us. Christ would not have died for us if God had not believed in our ability to respond in faith to His redeeming love. He is not a God of waste.

When our belief responds to God's believing power, a dynamic process of possibility toward change and growth occurs. At times the change is attitudinal toward mountains which are not moved; they remain, but we rise above them with changed attitudes. God's belief in us and our trust in Him, others, and ourselves cause us to stand on the mountains instead of being defeated by them.

A second change which often occurs in a believing community is the actual removal of mountains. At times the removal is immediate. We see evidence of this in the miracles of Jesus. When belief removes mountains in this manner, let us celebrate with gratitude God's ministry of restoration. When mountain moving is not immediate, however, let us not despair. For at that point two possibilities remain. One has already been mentioned. It is the possibility of faith's triumph through an attitude which causes the believer to stand undefeated on the mountains which remain. The other possibility is the removal of the mountain through a process of time and patience. This involves a willingness to take faith's "shovel" and to begin digging on one side of the mountain. Such digging occurs in a believing community where one hears the faith shovels of God and fellow believers at work in the mountain-moving process. Often this process involves the medical as well as the spiritual community where mountains are reduced in size instead of removed entirely.

This was the case with Gail's mountain. In a believing community he continued to dig away at his speech impediment. Progress was slow, and there were periods of discouragement. For example, I remember German classes when Gail would try for minutes to say a German vocabulary word. Then, shaking his head, he would request that the professor call on someone else. Gail continued to believe, however, in spite of the daily defeats. We continued to support him with our belief in a fellowship of mutual acceptance. We developed such a bond of trust that we were able to joke about Gail's impediment. It was that kind of closeness where we laughed with Gail at his mountain; he knew we were not laughing at him. Such closeness is a part of a believing community. In it, degree by degree, we observed the mountain moving.

The big challenge to our group's faith came during our senior year. My home church, the Northside Baptist Church of Rock Hill, South Carolina, invited some of us to lead in Sunday School and morning worship. The Baptist Student Union to which we belonged sponsored the weekend trip. When we arrived in Rock Hill, we had a planning session to assign responsibilities for the following

day. In that session, the various responsibilities were mentioned by our student leader. We either volunteered or
suggested someone we considered right for the assign-
ment.

With most of the responsibilities assigned, Ray Austin,
our student leader, said, "Who wants to be our presiding
officer for the morning worship service?" The group
became silent. We knew that was an important responsibility. No one seemed to want to volunteer. Suddenly Gail
broke the silence and said, "I'll preside if it's OK with the
rest of you." For a moment we said nothing. I think all of
us felt anxiety gnawing at our power to believe. We were
afraid that Gail might "freeze" and experience a public
defeat. Finally Ray asked, "How about it; what do you
think?" We gave Gail our vote of confidence.

That night we prayed for Gail. We knew that the next
day would be a test of his courage and our faith. After the
Sunday School hour, we gathered in the sanctuary for
morning worship. The building was completely filled with
people eagerly awaiting an experience of worship. Rever-
end Lewis McKinney, my home church pastor, stood, welcomed the people, and said, "I will now turn the
remainder of the worship time over to Mr. Gail Moul and
his fellow students from Furman University." Gail walked
to the pulpit and began to speak. For a moment we were
tense. Then we relaxed. Gail was speaking flawlessly.
From the beginning of the worship experience until the
end, he did not fumble a single word. As Gail presided, I
looked into the faces of people I had known all my life. I
saw their admiration for Gail. They were not aware, however, of the personal battle of faith which he had fought
all the way from Pearl Harbor to that moment in time.

When the worship service was over, our believing community came together at the front of the sanctuary. I wish

I could describe for you what we saw in Gail Moul's face that morning. Emotions too rich and too deep for words leaped out at us as he said, "We did it, fellows!" We had done it. It happened in a community of faith where God's belief in us and our belief in Him had caused us to live together in a mountain-moving fellowship.

Gail's mountain had not vanished. Its size had been reduced considerably, however, and Gail was standing on it. It had come to pass in a believing community.

# 2

# Come to the Table

## Goal
To develop a deeper awareness of the church as a family context. All of us have sat at family tables. God also has a table. He invites us to it. The Father's table is a family table. Using this goal for a Wednesday evening prayer service could prepare the church for approaching the Lord's table on Sunday.

## Scripture
Now as they were eating, Jesus took bread and blessed, and broke it, and gave it to the disciples and said, "Take, eat, this is my body." And he took a cup and when he had given thanks, he gave it to them saying, "Drink of it, all of you; for this is my blood of the covenant, which is poured out for many for the forgiveness of sins. I tell you that I shall not drink again of this fruit of the vine until that day when I drink it new with you in my Father's kingdom" (Matt. 26:26-29).

## The Church at Prayer
The worship leader can lead the church to:

1. Remember all of the tables at which they have been blessed. Prayer as gratitude can be offered.

2. Pray for those who have not claimed their place at the family table. This is prayer as intercession.

3. Prepare for coming to the Lord's table. This is prayer as commitment and confession.

15

I want to invite you to look in on a familiar scene; it is mealtime. People are together around a table. A writer says this about the gathering: Read Matthew 26:26-29.

An invitation to come and eat was extended to that group. Someone said, "Come to the table." Can you remember those words being spoken to you, "Come to the table"? You may have been upstairs and your mother or father said, "Come to the table; get out of bed you lazy head! You're going to be late for school. Come and get it while it's hot!" It may be that you were outside and someone threw the door open and said, "It's on the table!"

We all have these memories. Some of us who were the called ones are now the callers. We go and say to those upstairs, downstairs, or outside, "Come to the table; it's time to eat."

There are times when we come to the table for the breakfast meal. This is usually a hurried activity as we keep one eye on the table and one eye on the clock. There are other times when the call comes for lunch. But let's face it; lunch is no longer a family experience. The children are usually at school, and mother and father are at work or at home. But then there comes the call, "Come to the table," and it's dinner time. I wish I could say this is always a relaxed experience for the family. We know, however, that often the evening meal is a matter of coming in from busy schedules, eating hurriedly, and then the family scatters again to various outside activities. But, ever so often, there is that free night; may God preserve the free nights in order that the cohesiveness of the family might be maintained. With the free night, the invitation comes, "Come to the table!"

The family gathers. And once again we are in touch. We touch each other in at least two ways at the family table. First, we touch each other through fellowship and laughter. I remember one Saturday night when I was a child;

Saturday night was fellowship night for us, and during the winter months we had oyster stew and fried oysters. That particular night we were at the table. Mom had already placed before us a big pot filled with piping hot oyster stew from which steam was swirling toward the ceiling. Then she left the table for a moment to get an extra box of crackers from the pantry. The crackers had been in the pantry for some time. She returned to the table and opened the box. Then the fireworks began. A little mouse, captured in the box of crackers, jumped into Mom's bowl of oyster stew. As he jumped from the box to the bowl, Mom fell from her chair to the floor. After we gave the mouse a decent burial via the back door, and after we retrieved Mom from the floor, we had a beautiful time of fellowship and laughter.

Until this day, when we get together as the old family unit, someone will say, "Mom, do you remember that night long ago when you and the mouse entertained the family by seeing who could jump the fartherest?" Well, you see, these are memories. They are stored away in a special memory place. We call them forth as intimate talk about the table.

There's something else which happens at the table. We not only fellowship and laugh around the table. We also learn. There are times when children in the relaxed and spontaneous atmosphere of fellowship, love, and laughter, come forth with those significant questions and problems which are deep within them. Those are teachable moments—and how important they are! Family attitudes and values shape those young and open personalities in far-reaching ways. Someone said profoundly, "We learn our hates from the ones we love." We also learn how to love from those whom we love.

I recall how I learned the attitude of my father toward the family; it happened at the table. I knew he loved us, but I did not know the degree to which he loved his family. There was something special about our meal that day; it was Christmas. My oldest brother, Virgil, was in the South Pacific. The Second World War had taken him to that area of the world. We bowed our heads for the Christmas blessing. My father led us. When he tried to mention Virgil's name, his voice broke. He couldn't say it. He got up from the table, went into another room and cried. The absence of one of his children at the table made a vast difference; I knew how much my dad missed his son.

The following Christmas Virgil was at home. We were all together as a family around the table. I looked at my dad and saw in his eyes a radiant, settled expression of joy as he looked toward Virgil who was there. Then he said, "Virgil, will you lead us in the Christmas prayer?" A part of my father's attitude came to me because I shared his joy in the presence of my brother at the table.

"Come to the table!" And you see, Jesus teaches us that this is the way we are to feel toward this Being called God! He's not some abstract idea floating around in space. The apostle Paul said when you think of God and when you talk to Him, say, "Abba Father," which means intimate Father. And this is the One Who comes to invite us to a table which He has prepared.

One of the most tragic things in all the world is for someone to feel one does not belong at one's father's table; or, even more tragic, to feel that one does not want to be at the Father's table. I think I can understand those feelings, however. When I was a second grader, I got the feeling that I didn't belong to my family. I had heard the stories of my birth; they told me that when I was born I had red hair. When I looked in the mirror, however, I saw white hair. They called me "cottontop." I looked at my brother, Buddy, and he had dark hair. So did Virgil and my sister, Katherine. Why was I different? *Where in the world did I come from?* I thought. One day it all came out when I had an argument with my mother and father. I said to them, "I don't believe I belong to you anyway." In tears, I rushed to the bedroom. There I was and it was mealtime.

I had not been in the bedroom long when I heard the sound of footsteps. I knew they belonged to my dad. He sat down on the bed beside me. For a moment nothing was said. Then he started, "Frank, you know the room next to where you are." I didn't say anything, but he knew I was listening. He continued, "On May 1, 1935 your mother was in there in that bed. You hadn't been born." And then he added, "We knew it was time for your birth. I called Aunt Sally and Aunt Mary, and then your mother said, 'Arles, you had better call the doctor.' So I went after Dr. Frank Straight, after whom you were named. When he arrived I waited outside in the hall. From there I heard your first cry. You did have red hair. Aunt Mary was filled with joy because she had a son who had red hair, too." Then Dad said, "Frank, you were my son then, and you're my son now. I don't want to hear anymore of this stuff about not being my son!" He reached and took my arm and said, "Let's go to the table; it's ready." From that day until this I have never doubted that I was the son of my father.

God is also a Father. At the manger in Bethlehem He said to us, "You are mine by birth." And at the cross He said something vastly significant—"You are still mine," and that comes about through adoption. We are God's naturally by birth; we are also His by adoption into His family. From the cradle to the cross, into the resurrection God says, "You belong to me." And that's why He says to all of His created and redeemed sons and daughters, "Come to the table." Have you claimed your place at His family table?

# 3

# Finding Our Place

## Goal

To reemphasize the importance of places and persons in our lives, especially God Who is our dwelling place.

## Scripture

So we know and believe the love God has for us. God is love, and he who abides in love abides in God, and God abides in him (1 John 4:16).

## The Church at Prayer

The worship leader can lead the church to pray for people as they seek various places in life. Some are:

1. Children as they seek a place in school, nature, and among peers.

2. Teenagers as they seek a place of confidence with parents, friends, and themselves.

3. Singles as they seek their place in the world of persons.

4. Young adults as they seek a vocational and relational place in the adult world.

5. Mid and senior adults as they seek places of spiritual meaning in the peak and decline years of life.

John appeared at our house at about 2 PM one afternoon. He had an unusual request to make. "Pastor Frank," he said, "will you help me to get to the United States?" John and I had one thing in common. Both of us had come to Brazil from other countries. My family and I had arrived in Brazil in 1966 as Southern Baptist missionaries. John had come to Brazil in 1949 from Hungary. He had been exiled from his country by the Communist regime.

I listened intently as he shared his story. He had been a governmental official in Hungary. When the Communists came to power in his country, he lost his job and had to flee from his hometown. His family was imprisoned and never heard from again. Along with many others, John left his country in order to remain alive. Later he made his way to Brazil and had lived there for about seventeen years. Being in his late seventies, John's longings to have contact with home had intensified. The only member of his family alive, to his knowledge, was a nephew who had emigrated to the United States. That nephew represented to John a family, a home, and a place.

I tried to help John. But after talking with persons at the U. S. Embassy in Sao Paulo, I realized that John's chances of going to the United States were almost nil. He would have to have a solid promise of a job in the states before he could receive the necessary documents. I wrote to several friends in the United States about John. Their companies, however, did not need the liability of a man in the evening years of his human potential. John remained in Brazil, and I'm sure enjoyed a degree of happiness, for I found him to be a relational person. But his memories of significant persons and places, which are a part of the process of growing up and older, brought him pain. He was homesick for the places he remembered.

We identify with John. For a part of being human is seeking places in life. Paul Tournier in his book, *A Place for You,* speaks of this quest. According to Dr. Tournier, a Swiss doctor and devoted Christian, to be human is to seek places to be. What is this seeking process all about? It has to do with happiness, rest, creativity, fulfillment, acceptance, and appreciation. These human longings, and others, are attached to geographical, vocational, and relational places in our lives.

Geographical places shape our lives more than we may realize. This truth became quite real to me in the fall of 1977. My wife, Pat, and I had gone to Atlanta, Georgia, where our Georgia Baptist Convention was holding its annual meeting. In the midst of joyful fellowship, a message of grief came to us. My father had died about seven o'clock that morning. He had been ill with cancer for several years. We had gone through periods of anticipatory grief during the months of his decline. The actual death had finally come. After calling our children in Statesboro, Georgia, and arranging for them to travel with my wife's parents, Pat and I left Atlanta en route to Rock Hill, South Carolina, the place of our births.

Grief does a large portion of its healing work in the dimension of memory. We found that to be true for us as we traveled along Interstate 85. Around noon we passed through Greenville, South Carolina. Our grief and memory identified with that place. Both Pat and I had attended college there. She had gone to North Greenville Junior College. I had attended Furman University. In my grief I remembered my father's many sacrifices which had made possible my college education. Without his parental care, plus that of my mother, Greenville may have been just another piece of geography through which we passed thoughtlessly. But as we passed through that Piedmont city under a bright November sun, it was with a sense of homeness and being in place. The very geography, bound up in our common memories, reached out to comfort our wounded spirits.

From Greenville to Rock Hill we passed by sights which gave us a sense of being in place, also. Oak trees which grow tall like quiet sentinels, straw fields rimmed by honeysuckle thickets, red clay banks causing the landscape to blush with intermittent surprise, these geographical traits, and others, became nature's hand of comfort reaching out to touch us. We were not strangers in a distant place. The geography which had been our birth and growth place, became our minister as we made our way toward family and friends.

I can understand why the Jews from generation to generation have looked toward Jerusalem in times of tears, terror, and celebration. It has been and remains their geographical place. They are no different from us. Deep within us there is a need for a place, a place to be and with which we can identify human emotions. Surely God has put that longing there.

The longing, however, is not just geographical in nature. It is also vocational. We need a place to be vocationally. People speak of this need in various ways. At times someone will say, "I'm looking for my place in life." Or, someone may ask the question, "Where is my niche in life?" In this fashion we speak of our place, our place of being at home vocationally. There is nothing, I'm convinced, which can make a person happier than to have the feeling, "I've found my place in life."

A significant vocational place seeks to fulfill at least two human needs. First, there is the economic need. Our world functions according to economic principles and standards. There is nothing wrong with appropriate concern for economic advancement and justice in seeking one's vocational place. This should not be viewed as greed when based upon dedicated and honest services rendered. Much needs to be said and changed about what I choose to call the idolatry of certain occupations and professions. Why should some people be paid as though they were gods, while others give their vocational gifts with equal and sometimes greater dedication? Certainly when God's kingdom comes fully, such idolatry will cease. He will give our vocational places their proper value.

A second human need met in finding our vocational place is that of fulfilling our creative gifts. Here we must listen to the spirit within, the creative spirit. If the spirit of an artist, poet, singer, prophet, doctor, lawyer, etc., is within, we should release it through adequate preparation and dedication.

Children and young people should realize that arriving at their vocational place is both gift and achievement. The gift or gifts are in the form of raw materials and resources. The achievement comes from long hours of careful and dedicated preparation in which the raw materials become refined and ready for service. There are persons who never arrive at their vocational place because they see that place only as gift and not as a process of developmental growth.

The Book of Genesis reminds us that even God comes to His vocational place through both gift and process. He has the beautiful gift of creative power. The creation account states, however, that His spirit brooded over chaos and brought forth from it, at God's chosen pace, the creation. God's creativity was more than gift; it involved a process of becoming, an achievement.

So it is with us. Our human spirits brood over our inner space and see there the struggle between creation and chaos, form and formlessness. Vocational courage calls us to see the patterns of creativity within and to bring them forth as an act of vocational achievement. When such courage is rooted in self-giving love, our vocational place becomes a joyful place to be. It is joyful because, being created in God's image, we have a need to give that which is received, valued, appreciated, and shared by other persons. It is in such giving that we discover the meaning of fulfilled personhood.

I return now to my Hungarian friend. John missed his geographical and vocational places, to be sure. The main place for which he felt homesick, however, was his relational place. This is why, I'm sure, he wanted to see his nephew. He was his only living family relative. This does not mean that he had not established other significant friendships. He had. In old age, however, one returns to that relational place called family. John was doing a natural thing.

Again we identify with John. We have a place in the lives of people. That place ultimately gives meaning to both geography and vocations. If our relational place is creative and fulfilling, it can transform our physical surroundings and our vocational commitments and cause them to be happy places. Our relational place is ever with us; it is the ability to relate to other persons with accepting and creative interpersonal love.

Where does this ability originate? It comes from the creative, loving spirit of God. The universe in which we live is His relational place. We were invited by Him to live in it through relationships. Just as He created a place and populated it with persons to love and be loved by Him, we create our relational places and populate them with persons with whom we share the blessings of love and life.

The teenage period is a time of choosing our relational

place. During those growth years, much relational choosing is done. This is the meaning of choosing peer groups,
having sweethearts, going steady, transacting the engage-
ment, and, finally, getting married. These are choices
through which we establish the relational place which is
populated with chosen persons. Or, if we opt toward sin-
gleness, then our relational place is populated with chosen persons from the perspective of singlehood. However
we choose to create our relational place, we know that
deep within we are following the pattern of God's own
personhood.

The greatest truth about our longing for a place is this—
our most significant place is a person. The Bible puts it in
beautiful relational terms, "Lord, thou hast been our
dwelling place in all generations" (Ps. 90:1). This means
that when we know the meaning of self-giving love, we
are dwelling in an everlasting place which is a person.
For, "God is love, and he who abides in love abides in God,
and God abides in him" (1 John 4:16). To dwell in love
which knows how to give as blessing is to dwell in God.

John did not return to his relational place symbolized
by his nephew. He had access, however, to a person in
Whom he could abide in a foreign land. He knew the
Lord, Who is our place, our permanent place.

# 4

# The Joy of Your Name

### Goal
To recapture the importance of the family name which is given to us in the baptismal experience.

### Scripture
Go therefore and make disciples of all nations, baptizing them in the name of the Father and of the Son and of the Holy Spirit, teaching them to observe all that I have commanded you; and lo, I am with you always, to the close of the age (Matt. 28:19-20).

### The Church at Prayer
The worship leader can lead the church to:

1. Give gratitude for their earthly family names.

2. Claim the full meaning of the eternal Father's name being given through Jesus Christ to all of God's redeemed children.

3. Recommit itself to the task of sharing the family name with all people.

My wife, Pat, and I have had the joy of giving names to four children since our wedding in June 1957. Each birth holds an unforgettable place in the making of our family history.

Perri Lyn, our oldest child and only daughter, came to us early in our married life. Pat was teaching school while I was finishing my Bachelor of Divinity degree at Southeastern Baptist Theological Seminary at Wake Forest, North Carolina. We were living in a campus apartment building for childless couples when Pat became pregnant. There were four couples living on the floor where we lived. Suddenly, the "birth angel" began to visit our floor. The couple in the end apartment announced that they were expecting. Several weeks later the couple next to them said, "We're going to have a baby!" That left two other couples on the floor, Allen and Mozelle Wadsworth and us. From the two expecting couples we received a word of encouragement, "Come on and make it a clean sweep!" We were very cooperative. Before the semester ended, Allen and Mozelle and Pat and I had joined the ranks of the expecting ones. It had become a clean sweep!

Perri's birth came on July 23, 1959. I shall never forget waiting outside the delivery room for the arrival of our first child. I can still recall through imagery the nurses' station to the left, a bud vase containing a single red rose resting on the counter, and the clock just beside the swinging doors racing toward midnight. About 11:45 the doors opened. A nurse came toward us carrying a baby wrapped in a blanket. She said, "Mr. Hawkins, you have a little girl." She was very special to Pat and me. We named her Perri Lyn after a young lady named Perri Seigel. Pat and I had admired Perri when she was a teenager and we were children. We thought she was beautiful.

Her name seemed to fit our daughter. To us, she was beautiful, also.

Greg was the second child to bless our family. He came after I had graduated from seminary. We had moved to Edgemoor, South Carolina, where I became pastor of the Harmony Baptist Church. Our church family shared our joy in anticipating the birth of our second child. Greg decided he would be a Sunday baby. About 3:00 AM on Sunday, November 12, 1961, Pat began to have birth pains. I drove her with care to York General Hospital, in our hometown, Rock Hill, South Carolina. There, our first son was born about 7:30 AM. After viewing our baby and sharing some time with Pat, I drove back to our church for Sunday School and worship. I'm not sure about the quality of my sermon that morning. There was such joy in my heart, however, that if I had read from the dictionary, I believe it would have been inspirational!

We gave to our first son the name, Franklin Gregory. The name, Franklin, came from his father who had been named after the doctor who delivered him, Dr. Franklin Strait. Gregory was the name we gave him to mark his own unique personhood. He was to be called "Greg."

Before Greg left the diaper stage, we were in the process of saying "welcome" to our third child. Todd came at a time of transition for our family. A church in the foothills of the Smoky Mountains, the First Baptist Church of Old Fort, North Carolina, had invited me to be their pastor. I accepted their invitation just weeks before Todd was to be born. Although we moved our household belongings to Old Fort, Pat and the children remained in Rock Hill with her parents. She did not want to change doctors in the ninth month of pregnancy. I commuted between Rock Hill and Old Fort until Todd's birth.

Todd decided to be a Monday baby. After the Sunday

evening service on April 14, 1963, I left Old Fort and drove home to be with Pat, Perri, and Greg. About midnight Pat nudged me and said, "Frank, wake up, my pains are getting closer together!" After two experiences with birth, I had learned that Pat was not given to "false alarms." We rushed to the hospital and began the waiting period. Fortunate for me, a good friend of ours, Mrs. Saunders, was on nursing duty that night. She had known Pat and me since childhood. Mrs. Saunders became my guardian angel that night. She said, "Frank, you look beat; go lie down and when Pat is ready to deliver, I'll call you." My weary body moved obligingly to a hospital bed where I rested until Mrs. Saunders' excited voice interrupted my slumber. She said, "Frank, Pat's going to deliver soon!" I rushed to the waiting room, where, after about an hour, I received the joyful news, "Your baby boy and wife are doing fine!"

We named our third child, Gary Todd. The name Gary had no family significance. It just had a good sound to us. The name to which our son would answer, Todd, came from his father's love of history. I recalled from my college history classes that Abe Lincoln had a son named Todd. Pat and I liked the name. It blended well with the short, solid names of our other children.

After Todd was born, we thought our family was complete. And, yet, we had in store for us the joy of naming a fourth child. Brad came fourteen years later. We had experienced several vocational sojourns in the meantime. From Old Fort, North Carolina, we had gone to Sao Paulo, Brazil, as Southern Baptist missionaries. After a term in Brazil, we returned to Louisville, Kentucky in 1970, where I became pastor of the Melbourne Heights Baptist Church. After four years of creative growth and service there, I accepted the call to become pastor of the First Baptist Church of Statesboro, Georgia.

When we left Louisville, our family experienced acute grief. We had grieved when we had left other places, also. But Louisville had been the place where our children had become teenagers. Perri and Greg had had their first dates there. Todd had reached age twelve and was on the verge of the teenage explosion. Their grief in leaving sweethearts and peer groups intensified the grief which Pat and I felt in leaving a place and a people to which we had become attached emotionally. Our experience was not unique, however. We were experiencing what countless persons encounter in our highly mobile society.

One statement which Perri made in the midst of her transitional grief proved to be prophetic. She said to Pat one day while we were attempting to sell our house, "Mother, I wouldn't mind moving to Statesboro if you were pregnant." Perri's comment provided us a moment of laughter which gave relief to our pain in leaving. A year later, we fulfilled Perri's wish. Pat became pregnant with Brad. Our new church family entered the expectant mood of the Hawkins family. Our joy became their joy. Pastors and their families are blessed by such church communities which share their joys and sorrows in terms of mutual support.

Brad was born on December 29, 1976. Perri, Greg, and Todd, for whom I had waited as father and for whom Pat had given her physical self as the special human place of their birth, waited with me until Brad was brought to us from the delivery room. The joy in my heart, and in Pat's heart as well, was made complete because Brad was accepted by his sister and brothers as a blessed gift.

We named our fourth child Bradley Stewart. Stewart was a family name; Pat's mother had been a Stewart before marriage. Bradley would be his given name of identification. Like Perri, Greg, and Todd, he would give to that chosen name his own unique meaning as a created and creative person. Our family was now complete!

In birthing children and in giving them names, Pat and I have discovered some traces of the meaning of Christian personhood in the redeemed family of God. Just as we gave names to our children when they were born, we receive names when we experience birth through faith and grace into God's redeemed family. Baptism symbolizes in dynamic fashion this name-giving inclusion into a new family context. When the minister says, "I baptize you in the name of the Father, the Son and the Holy Spirit," he is not speaking idle words. In that moment he symbolizes through those words a new identity and identification through name giving and reception.

In fact, Christian baptism speaks of the giving of two names by a Father to His new family members. First, we receive the name of our Father. Just as an earthly father gives his name to his children at birth, God the Father gives to His redeemed children His eternal name as an act of blessing and grace. Second, just as we receive a given name from earthly parents, we also receive a given name from God the Father. That name is Christian. This becomes the given name of our identity and identification as family members. This is why the words, "I baptize you in the name of the Father, the Son, and the Holy Spirit," are central to the meaning of Christian baptism; they speak of a Father's joy in sharing a family name and a given name with new family members.

In the baptismal experience of Jesus we see something of the blessed meaning which can exist between parent and child. When God viewed His Son in that moment of their family relationship, He said of Jesus, "This is my beloved Son, with whom I am well pleased" (Matt. 3:17). The meaning of God's redemptive love is revealed in those words. Through His Son, God the Father continues to speak over the baptism of His new family members; "These are my beloved sons and daughters in whom I am well pleased." The meaning of divine grace is that the same family love which exists between God the Father and the Son is ours in being included in His redeemed family. It is ours to receive and to share with family brothers and sisters.

What a joy it is, therefore, to recognize that through Christ He names us and invites us to a family table and shares with us all of the rights, privileges, and responsibilities of family members. After all, isn't this the meaning of birth into a family? We receive a name, a place at our parents' table, and family rights and responsibilities.

The deep significance of our Father's joy came to me when I led Greg and Todd in their baptismal experience. After I spoke the words, "I baptize you, my brothers, in the name of the Father, the Son, and the Holy Spirit," I realized that I had to leave the parental level and accept them as brothers in the family of the Father of us all. In God's family we transcend all family roles in accepting through faith an everlasting family name which is both blessing and responsibility.

Perri was baptized by our Brazilian pastor when we were missionaries in Brazil. Her baptism brought to Pat and me the same recognition of a new family identification.

# 5

## Keeping and Sharing Secrets

### Goal

To lead the church to an appreciation of the place of secrets in human and spiritual growth.

### Scripture

The secret things belong to the Lord our God; but the things that are revealed belong to us and to our children for ever (Deut. 29:29).

### The Church at Prayer

The worship leader can:

1. Lead the church to express gratitude for God's revealed secrets. The apostle Paul speaks of God sharing His secrets in Ephesians 1. In Christ, God makes known the good secrets of His will and grace.

2. Guide the church to an awareness of their secrets. To have secrets is to be like our Heavenly Father. As humans, however, our secrets are both good and bad. The sharing of good secrets is self-disclosure as love. The sharing of bad secrets is confession for the purpose of obtaining forgiveness and help. The former is gift sharing. The latter is grace receiving. If one does not share good secrets, one is not in touch with gifts. If one does not share bad secrets with God and responsible and trusted others, forgiveness cannot become a healing reality.

It is no secret that at birth you and I possess no secrets. Before birth we belong to the abdominal world of mother where dependence on her body system is a matter of survival. After birth we still belong to mother's world. Our identity is satellite to hers. Father stands by in the wing area of personhood; he is to nurture mother as she nurtures the children. In such an infantile state we have no secrets to keep and share.

The development of secrets, however, as Paul Tournier points out in his book, *Secrets,* is a healthy and normal part of spiritual and personality growth. Stage by stage children develop their own individuality in terms of rights related to secrets.

A very early stage of secrecy, which we remember well, comes when children begin to play with other children. Through imagination they form and fashion their own secret territory. They may take on the identity of fairy tale personalities. At times their fantasy ability leads them to high adventure in outer space or on some distant island where treasure is found and shared. It is not uncommon for children to create imaginary friends at this stage, especially when there is a shortage of available playmates their own age. In this fashion children develop their own individuality by having an imagined world in which secrets are shared and kept with other children. In doing this, children communicate to their parents a very beautiful message which says, "We, too, are persons with the right to keep and share secrets." I feel sure Jesus had childlike imagination in mind when He said, "Truly, I say to you, whoever does not receive the kingdom of God like a child shall not enter it" (Luke 18:17).

When children reach the school stage, their capacity for secrets reveals a reorientation away, but not entirely, from fantasy roles toward real friendship roles. They begin to keep their little secrets with special friends and sweethearts. Often their secrets are not shared with mother and father. I remember one mother who asked her seven-year-old son the question, "Do you have a sweetheart?" He mumbled an unclear response to her as he turned away. Several days later in a conversation with June's mother, she discovered that her son not only claimed June as his sweetheart, but had two others for good measure. That mother could have panicked and said to herself, "My son is keeping things from me; what will I do?" Instead, she accepted her son's response as a compliment. He was communicating to her and his father a very clear growth message which said, "Mom and Dad, I'm growing up and I can handle some things for myself." He was doing a very healthy and normal thing which suggested his awareness of his own identity as a maturing, choosing person. Maturing parents can accept that awareness on the part of their children and give to it both growing room and structured boundaries.

In late childhood, secrets grow with personality development. At this stage, children begin to have language secrets. New words enter their vocabulary which have special meaning to a select group of peer friends. At times, they develop a secret language which permits them to talk and not be understood by parents and nongroup people.

In my early ministry, I witnessed two preadolescents as they used their secret language. I had been invited to speak in a rural church near Newberry, South Carolina. After the morning service, I went to a lovely country house as the guest of Mr. and Mrs. Smith. The Smiths had two daughters; both were in late childhood. We enjoyed a delicious meal and then, country-style, entered a spacious living room for unhurried conversation. Then it happened. Betty and Beth began to talk in a language which was foreign to me. After trying to penetrate their secrets, I asked Mrs. Smith, "What are your girls saying?" "Oh," she replied, "they are saying something they don't want us to understand." Mrs. Smith went on to tell me about their secret language. By mixing up consonants and vowels in a rhythmic pattern understandable to them, they had created a language all their own. With it they could keep and share sister secrets. Mr. and Mrs. Smith were not threatened by their daughters' secret language. They viewed their girls' secrets as a part of their emerging individuality.

When children reach their teen years, secrets become a part of a natural emotional movement away from childhood dependence toward adult independence. In early adolescence a form of declaring independence is through territorial relocation. This can happen in part when a teenager says, "Mom and Dad, can I have the junk room at the end of the hall for my room?" What is he asking for? He is seeking for life space where he can begin to transact independence. Usually the room is decorated with pictures, posters, names, and slogans which mean very little to his parents. But to him and his friends, each item has meaning which speaks of their growing independence.

Secrecy at this age begins to take on the meaning of interpersonal communication. This happens in at least three forms—telephoning, writing letters, and dating. The advent of teenage telephoning has been the subject of many heated family discussions; "What do you have to talk about which takes so long?" mother inquires. "Oh, just stuff," comes the answer. Sometimes teenagers are known to just breathe at each other on the phone for five or ten minutes. A very natural process is happening, however, They are declaring their independence along acceptable "lines."

Writing letters which are stuffed in blue jean pockets and notebooks is another form of secrecy as emerging interpersonal communication growth. These letters are not usually shared with parents. They are a part of the teenagers' quest for independence. Maturing parents tend to see that process taking place in their sons and daughters and maintain a close but guarded distance from a beautiful and natural drama being enacted before their eyes. If parents sense that their teenagers are headed toward destructive patterns of secrecy, however, their sense of responsibility will cause them to reach out to help. This should not be done in Sherlock Holmes detective style where parents spy on their children. It should be done honestly as an open agenda. Teenagers understand and appreciate this kind of face-to-face truthfulness.

The most serious form of interpersonal communication which occurs in adolescence is dating. The secrets of dating are both wonderful and crucial. Parents and teenagers realize this and view dating as the process which moves persons from the family of one's birth to the family of one's own choosing. Trusting teenagers to their dating secrets and being trustworthy with dating secrets is not a quick decision made just before the first date. The trust-trustworthy partnership begins in early childhood and continues all the way to safe arrival in the kingdom of responsible and free adult relationships. In this partnership there should be a proper balance between over protection which tends to view human secrets as dangerous and overpermissiveness which views all secrecy as "nobody else's business." Both extremes can keep an emerging person from becoming a free, choosing, and responsible adult, which is the goal of parenthood.

When the secrets of personhood are experienced as a healthy and natural process of establishing one's own individuality, then dating becomes an exciting time of interpersonal sharing. The end result becomes the sharing of life's most intimate secrets, the secrets of human sexuality, experienced by two people who are free to open the secrets of their personhood to each other in responsible marriage.

Persons fortunate enough to grow up in such a family atmosphere of trust and trustworthiness tend to become parents who can guide their children in both keeping and sharing the secrets of human growth. And where do we receive this gift of keeping and sharing secrets? We receive it from God, our Father. Before the creation, He possessed the eternal secrets of His own personhood. Because He was a person, however, He came out of secrecy and gave Himself in creation and redemption. In His image we, too, possess the gift of secrets, which being gift, needs to be given in a process of responsible becoming.

# 6

# Thoughts from Sand and Sea

### Goal
To renew the childlike and wonder dimension of the church. This needs to be reborn in us at various ages during the human journey.

### Scripture
Truly, I say to you, whoever does not receive the kingdom of God like a child shall not enter it (Luke 18:17).

### The Church at Prayer
The worship leader can:

1. Lead each person present to get in touch with the "child" within. We never cease being children with a God-given capacity to laugh, cry, look with wonder at the creation, and receive humbly what our Father wants to give freely.

2. Lead the church to celebrate the gift of God, self, and others with childlike joy.

3. Lead the church to pray for the gift of a flexible rhythm between the responsible execution of commitments to God and others, and the sheer enjoyment of God, others, and the good creation.

It happened during the summer of 1952. Lee, Don, and Steve invited me to go with them to Myrtle Beach for the weekend. Our senior year at Rock Hill High School was just weeks away. *Why not one last fling with Myrtle before school starts,* we thought. We stuffed our weekend gear in Steve's Oldsmobile and left Rock Hill en route to South Carolina's coast.

The August rains had already begun. That didn't dampen our spirits, however. We were familiar with the rapid entrance and exit of summer rains in South Carolina, especially in the month of August. But we felt sure that the beach would have its share of sunny hours.

Steve's car carried us swiftly by green fields where watermelons, corn, peaches, and tobacco had ripened under a palmetto sun. Already there was a hint of decline on the face of nature: a wrinkle or two which seemed to say, "The effortlessness of autumn is near."

Suddenly green and brown gave way to Atlantic blue. There it was before us, a multitude of openness we call the Atlantic Ocean. At that moment I remembered the first time I saw the ocean. It was at Beaufort, South Carolina, in the winter of 1942. My mother, father, brother, sister, sister-in-law, and I had gone there to visit my brother, Virgil, who was in boot training at the Parris Island Marine Base. Although I was only seven years old at the time, it was love at first sight. Something deep within me felt kinship with whatever is deep within the character and soul of an ocean. There was no sense of possessiveness, no desire to absorb or be absorbed, just a quiet feeling of touching and being touched by something which stretches the human spirit and calls it forth to its own creative potential. It was now ten years later but my love affair with the ocean was still on.

We hurriedly checked in at one of Myrtle Beach's many

dwellings for sea lovers. Of course, Myrtle Beach 1952 was nothing like Myrtle Beach today. Myrtle Beach today is an empire by the sea with international fame. For example, when spring comes, Myrtle and her beaches experience an invasion from Canadians migrating south to thaw out from an Arctic winter. Myrtle Beach 1952 however, was a simple lady who appealed mostly to South Carolinians and some other vacationing Americans.

It didn't take long to shed our jeans and take on the dress appropriate for children at play in sand and sea. I say children for a good reason. The ocean has a way of bringing out the child in most of us. Maybe that's why we go there from our structured world of role responsibility. The ocean has a way of leveling us to one size, that of children. Suddenly the family, professional, and social roles are gone as we feel sand between our toes and sea air pushing our hair in unpredictable directions. Can it be that playing in the ocean with the abandonment of a child is a form of God's soul therapy? Can it be one of God's places where inner healing can happen quietly and unnoticed as heavy roles are temporarily lifted?

That weekend during the summer of 1952 was different for me. I had promised my mother I would not overexpose myself to the sun and water. For I had been ill and my energies were still being recreated within my body. Keeping my contract with Mom, I occasionally left the fun of wrestling with the breakers to Lee, Don, and Steve, while I waded restfully in ankle-deep water.

As I walked in free solitude, the sea became my sanctuary. There was no choir; only the voices of wind and water. No one lifted a voice in sermonic utterance. A message came, however, a nonverbal message which found me waiting and open. First, there was a question, *What is life?* Then the answer followed, an answer which came as a gift, *'Tis but the ebbing of the tide of human existence upon the shores of time, where sands of souls are dropped momentarily and then are ushered back into the vast ocean of eternity.*

The gift had been given; it was mine now, forever. *We are deposited here,* I thought, *by unseen but loving hands which never cease to touch us.* I felt touched in that moment and I experienced the capacity, perhaps like a child, to touch a human face which touches back with a smile. I felt engulfed by a smile if that is possible—the smile of the Creator etched on the visible side of His creation.

Behind moistened eyes I found myself saying, "Thank You, God, for being here. Thank You for finding me even when I was not looking for You. Thank You for being in this multitude of openness. Thank You, God, for sending the tide of human existence and for being there to receive us when our time touches eternity."

From behind me a voice came, "Wake up, Frank." Don was headed toward me on an incoming wave. I laughed and fell half on the float and half on him. Once again I was at play with my friends.

That afternoon we left the beach and headed inland toward home, family, our last year of high school, college, and adult roles beyond. There, by the ocean, however, an encounter had occurred. In freeing my inner child to play, I had encountered the Person who had made my love affair with the ocean possible.

Suddenly I knew the meaning of Jesus' words, "Whoever does not receive the kingdom of God like a child shall not enter it." It is the childlikeness within us which can see and appreciate the Father within and beyond all things. This makes every event, even walking by the sea, a doorway into His kingdom.

# 7

# Discerning God's Will for You

### Goal
To assist the church as it seeks God's will in decision-making matters. Just as the church makes decisions and wants to be guided by God's will, the individual Christian makes decisions and wants to be guided by God's wisdom.

### Scripture
And Moses said, "I will turn aside and see this great sight, why the bush is not burnt" (Ex. 3:3).

### The Church at Prayer
The possibilities for collective praying concerning God's will are numerous. The worship leader can:

1. Build a relational bridge from Moses and Horeb to Christ and Gethsemane. The Old and New Testaments call us to pray, seeking God's will. Moses and our Lord model for us the quest to know His will.

2. Call the church to serious seeking for God's will concerning current challenges (i.e., church budget, Youth Week, etc.).

3. Direct individuals to prayer for God's will in human decisions (i.e., selecting the right college and career, making inspired decisions about marriage and family, etc.).

4. Guide the church to seek the mind of Christ concerning moral and ethical concerns in personal and community living.

One Sunday morning in 1964 I preached a sermon at the First Baptist Church, Old Fort, North Carolina, entitled, "Discerning God's Will for My Life." Later, as the worshipers were leaving the sanctuary, a Junior boy appeared before me and said, "Preacher, I listened to your sermon, but I have a question. How can I know God's will from my will?"

That question excited me for two reasons. First, Kenny had listened to my message; that's always a gift which a minister receives with delight! Second, he gave me an opportunity to move from being a preacher to being his pastor. This, too, is a gift which I receive with joy. I would much rather the congregation leave from worship with questions to be answered than exit in an attitude of complacent satisfaction.

The excitement of Kenny's question motivated me to renewed meditation about God's will. How can we discern God's will for our lives? How can a Junior boy or girl discern God's will for his or her life? In my mind I made a journey to one of the mountains of the Old Testament, Mount Horeb—the mountain of God. It is located between Palestine and Egypt in the area of the Sinai Peninsula. There, via holy Scripture, I heard a conversation between two persons in which one discerned the will of the other. Come with me to that mountain event.

Moses stands before a mystery—a burning bush which is not consumed. In it and through it he encounters the living God. God addresses Moses and shares with him the purpose of his life—the reason of his existence. He was born with potential gifts of leadership. Now God challenges Moses to bring these gifts to bear upon a people's deliverance from bondage. Moses must respond to the divine challenge.

In some form or fashion, this is a universal situation.

God has a "burning bush" for every person created in His image. He speaks His will; we respond. What happened on the mountain between God and Moses, therefore, is ultimately significant for us today. Three truths from the mountain of God will aid us as we think of our own "burning bush."

The first truth is this— *God revealed His will to Moses in spite of the negative circumstances which Moses had brought upon his life.* (The idea is from Leslie Weatherhead's book, *The Will of God.*) It is easy for us to view the burning bush episode as an event too lofty for us mortals to reach. There, we conjecture, a perfect God revealed a perfect will to an almost perfect man. In reality, however, Moses was strikingly similar to us. Let me explain what I mean.

Moses was born into the home of Hebrew slaves. The Hebrews had struggled in servitude for over three hundred years. To be sure, they prayed for deliverance. The heavens, however, appeared to be as insensitive as wrought iron. God could have sent a battalion of angels to smite the Egyptians. He could have prepared a convoy of ships to meet the Hebrews at the base of the Nile Delta. Instead, He chose to accomplish His will through a person. In fact, God usually implements His purposes through persons. That person was Moses. Shortly after birth, Moses was adopted into the household of Pharoah. He had the cultural and educational benefits of the Egyptian civilization. At the same time, he had his mother as his personal "Day and Night Care Center." He grew toward fulfilling God's will for his life. He did not know what that purpose was at the time. The Hebrews and Egyptians did not see him as a deliverer. Through historical retrospect, however, we can see this truth. His gifts were being prepared for vocational service.

But wait! Disaster struck. One day, in a moment of hot anger, Moses murdered an Egyptian taskmaster. Then he ran into the desert. He was banished from Egypt and the people whom he was to deliver. "How sad," we are apt to say. Moses had a solid future before him. But then he "goofed." He failed. It's all over. He has disappeared into the desert of defeat.

You and I can identify with Moses. We were born with purpose. Our faith teaches us that all human life is included in the arena of divine purpose. The will of God seeks to express itself through all persons. We grow toward rendering our gifts in service to God and man. Then it happens. We goof. We bring upon ourselves negative circumstances. And then, like Moses, we tend to flee from God into some spiritual desert of defeat. There it is easy to begin to think of God's will in the past tense—as something we almost reached but missed.

The burning bush, however, explodes the erroneous grammar of God's will in the past tense. God spoke to Moses in the present tense. He spoke to Moses about the future, not the past. Sure Moses goofed. Sure we fail. God is a Person, however, Who specializes in transforming deserts of defeat into burning bushes of new destiny. If we are to find God's will for our lives, it must be done in spite of the negative circumstances we have thrust upon ourselves. In the midst of those circumstances He does not abandon us; He meets us there, redemptively.

The second truth which speaks to us from Mount Horeb is this—*God revealed His will to Moses in the context of a spiritual courtship.* I chose these words carefully. Viewing the burning bush experience superficially, we are apt to think of a man who communicated anew with God after forty years of silence. I see the God and Moses scene differently; I see a man who ran to the land of Midian and, for forty years, was in quest of God. He communed with God in the quiet pastureland. God and Moses were involved in a spiritual courtship!

All of us are familiar with the process of courtship. It is a movement in the dynamics of interpersonal communication toward intimacy, devotion, and mutual surrender. The process begins with what I choose to call the "glance stage." This is when a boy glances at a girl and she glances back. The glance stage communicates the feeling, "I'm interested in you." The second level of courtship can be called the "group stage." In this stage glances give way to a desire which says, "I want to see you and know you up close." Group courting finally reaches the "dating stage." Communication at this point is intensified and often moves by way of "going steady" to the stage of mutual commitment. This is the burning bush moment in the process of courtship. It is when a man says to a woman, "I love you and want to share my life with you in the deepest possible intimacy." At this point two wills become one through commitment and surrender. The marital relationship which follows is a test of the quality of that commitment.

On Mount Horeb a process of spiritual courtship arrived at a moment of possible commitment of two selves and two wills to the deepest possible devotion and intimacy. God and Moses had moved through various stages of interpersonal communication. Now the question remained, "Would their wills be joined by the same holy covenant which marked God's relationship to Abraham and Isaac?"

This question brings us to the third truth which comes from the mountain of God. *In revealing His will to Moses, God expected personal surrender.* Two persons who commit themselves to each other in the covenant of marriage expect such surrender; it is mutual surrender of two wills out of which common dreams and purposes are achieved. Bowed before God, Moses sought to evade surrender. After all, he thought, *Who am I to lead the Hebrews out of bondage?* Moses tried to ignore the vocational gifts within him. This issue, however, stands at the heart of discerning God's will for one's life. Commitment to God's will always means surrender of one's gifts to God's redemptive work. Moses must not "cop out." He must bring what he is and has to the holy covenant. Before the burning bush, Moses surrendered himself to God. In that commitment the divine will and the will of Moses became one. In that will Moses found both peace and the meaning of his life.

The question I leave with you is this, "Where are you in your spiritual courtship with God?" The exciting truth which reaches us from the experience of Moses is this— the courtship can be transformed into a covenant of two wills which is shared out of devotion. Like Kenny, we are at a particular stage of courtship with God. Whatever that stage is, God invites us to discern His will in a process of interpersonal commitment.

# 8

# Be Angry and Sin Not

### Goal
To open the church as a place for resolving anger.

### Scripture
Be angry but do not sin; do not let the sun go down on your anger (Eph. 4:26).

### The Church at Prayer
The worship leader can lead the church to:

1. Be aware of its anger. If God gets angry (and the Bible says He does), then we, too, will get angry. Paul said it doesn't have to be sin, however.

2. Confess its anger. Not letting the sun go down on one's anger means to deal with it quickly—confess it, resolve it, bring it to our relationship with God and the one toward whom we feel anger.

3. Seek help for anger which is significantly hurting relationships in life. To "bottle up" anger can harm relationships by producing depression. To "blast" another verbally or physically can harm marriages and children. When these things happen, anger has become sin. In prayer we can bring our anger to Christ and to His power to transform it away from destruction toward reconciliation.

Somewhere in our common background, we have picked up the notion that anger is a negative human emotion. My hunch is that the idea has come, in part, from destructive forms of anger we have witnessed in others and experienced in ourselves.

In my circle of childhood friends, there was a boy whose anger I feared. He was constantly at war with someone in our peer group. One day while we were playing softball in a field close to our neighborhood, his anger got the best of him and he began to beat up on a kid smaller than he. Without his knowing it, his father saw what was happening. Johnny's father entered their house and then reappeared carrying something in his hand. It was a piece of rubber hose about three feet long. When he reached Johnny, he began to beat him with the piece of hose. Johnny screamed as he ran toward home. He continued to scream as his father beat him in their house.

Years later, in reflecting on that experience, I understood better Johnny's agressive behavior. He was a very angry young fellow. He had lived with parental anger which was destructive, and it was only natural for him to pass along to others what he had received at home.

Of course, anger does not have to be so exaggerated to be destructive. This was true for one family which came to me for counseling. The parents' major concern was Joan, their attractive sixteen-year-old daughter. She had become rebellious and had threatened to leave home. The parents were at their wits' end. In one of our counseling sessions, I asked Joan why she was so angry with her parents. She didn't waste any time revealing her feelings. According to her, she had become the family maid. Even though her mother did not have an outside job, she expected Joan to do the ironing and cooking for the family, along with other household duties. I asked her mother

about Joan's family report. She said, "It's true; I do expect
her to do the ironing and cooking. After all, she is our
daughter." Then I inquired, "Do you and Joan share the
ironing and cooking?" "No," she answered. "I had to do
it when I was her age and now she'll do it, just like I did."
For about fifteen minutes Joan's mother shared with me
what she had to do as a teenager in her home. After she
finished, I asked her, "How did you feel about having that
kind of responsibility as a teenager?" Her answer was
interesting. She said, "I didn't like it but I did it."

The family dynamics became clear. Joan's mother was
still angry with her parents about her teenage responsibilities. As a parent, she had refocused that anger toward
her own daughter. Her anger had called forth anger in
Joan. Mother and daughter were fighting a battle which
both would lose; their anger was damaging their relationship.

Because negative feelings are usually associated with
anger, it is easy for us to shy away from it as though it were
our enemy. The Bible teaches us, however, that anger can
be our ally in terms of blessings. In Ephesians 4:26 *a* we
are told, "Be angry but do not sin." In other words, anger
can be experienced without being a sin. It becomes sin
when we hide it and let it transform itself into settled
aversion which we call hate. If we follow the instructions
of the Bible, however, we will move our anger in another
direction, the direction of relationship building. The Bible
puts it this way, "Do not let the sun go down on your
anger" (Eph. 4:26 *b*). The meaning is clear. When we con-
ceal anger from others and ourselves and let it lurk within
us, it becomes our enemy. As our enemy, it works to bring
harm to our own physical and emotional health, and,
beyond that, it becomes a destructive force in the world

of interpersonal relationships. This was the case with Joan and her mother.

The relationship building side of anger comes when we experience anger as being a normal human emotion. Being a normal emotion, the Bible encourages us to own our anger and express it appropriately. There are, I believe, three steps in a biblically oriented expression of anger.

First, anger must be experienced as anger in our bodies. For years I experienced anger without giving my body the right to have such an emotion. Finally, in a sharing group, I was able to own my anger as mine. I began to be aware of what my anger did to my body; it gave me a churning sensation in the pit of my stomach. Your anger may affect you differently. Self-awareness at the point of experiencing anger is important. Without it, our anger usually owns us.

Once we can own our anger as being rightfully ours, we can begin the process of decision making. This is what the Bible means by not letting the sun go down on our anger. When we experience it as rightfully ours, we own it instead of it owning us. Then, that very day, we can express our anger which we control. This makes decision making possible, and, as a result, we begin to ask questions such as, "Who am I angry with? What has he or she done to make me angry? How shall I communicate my feelings of anger appropriately to those involved in my anger?"

Owning our anger and deciding how we shall express it leads to the third step in relationship-building anger. At this stage we bring our anger "to" our relationships instead of "against" our relationships. It is revealing that Jesus owned His anger in such a redemptive manner. He became angry with Simon Peter when Simon told Him He would not die on the cross. Jesus told Simon he was playing the role of Satan in doing that (Matt. 16:21-23). The crucial point we must not forget is that Jesus was angry "with" Simon not "against" him. He rebuked His disciple because He loved him, not because He hated him.

We also must choose how we will negotiate anger at the human level. The choice is not between getting angry and not getting angry. The choice is between destructive anger and constructive anger.

Dr. David Mace, past professor of family sociology, Bowman Gray School of Medicine, Winston-Salem, North Carolina, speaks of a practical formula we can use in sharing our anger in relationship building.[1] The formula begins with an acknowledgment of our anger as being anger. This is when we look toward the person with whom we are angry and say, "I'm angry with you." Acknowledgment is honesty; this is the beginning of a constructive handling of our anger. Acknowledgment is to be followed by the clarification stage. At this point we let the person know we are angry with him. We say, "The reason I am angry with you is this." Finally, acknowledgment and clarification are followed by mending. The mending motive is expressed by such thoughts as, *I don't want to be angry with you; help me to deal with it now.*

In this practical way we can be angry and not sin by dealing with our anger before the sun goes down. Constructive anger brings itself to relationships with the possibilities of forgiveness and reconciliation. There is no reason why we cannot be "in anger" with persons just as we are "in love" with persons. In this way, anger can serve the purposes of Christian love.

---

1. These thoughts were shared at a Christian Life Conference in Louisville, Kentucky in 1974.

# 9

# Leaving and Cleaving

## Goal

To make the church more aware of a beautiful process which leads to responsible and mature marital relating. This service could be prepared as a marriage renewal experience.

## Scripture

Therefore a man leaves his father and his mother and cleaves to his wife, and they become one flesh (Gen. 2:24).

## The Church at Prayer

The worship leader can:

1. Call the church to serious prayer for the strengthening of marriages.

2. Lead the church to pray for parents as they assist children to leave home with love, courage, and faith.

3. Guide the church to undergird leaving as a process which begins in childhood. Trust and care must work together in the church and in the home.

4. Lead the church to pray that cleaving in marriage be based upon mature and responsible love which is willing to forgive and grow.

Sue and Joe stood before me in the sanctuary of our church. Their faces communicated the joy they felt as they shared their wedding experience with family and friends. Bright candles, subdued chandeliers, well-chosen floral patterns, and excited wedding attendants provided a balanced context for the celebration scene.

After a prayer of invocation, I looked to Sue's father and asked the question, "Who gives Sue to be married to Joe?" Mr. Bennett answered with proud emotion, "Her mother and I do." Once he had spoken the words of parental consent, Mr. Bennett left Sue by Joe's side and took his place with Mrs. Bennett. It seemed to be a simple part of the wedding ritual. And yet, in a dynamic sense, those words, "Her mother and I do," were crucially important. They symbolized a beautiful process which the Bible speaks of as "leaving and cleaving." "Therefore a man leaves his father and his mother and cleaves to his wife, and they become one flesh" (Gen. 2:24).

When did the leaving process begin for Joe and Sue? It began when they were children. Degree by degree their parents gave them the freedom to leave. This was true as they left home to play with other children. It was true when they left for the first time to go to school. They experienced the freedom of leaving in attending summer camps, overnight stays in the homes of special friends. In these and other ways, their parents communicated to them a message of trust which said, "We believe in your ability to grow up and choose your own way in life."

In childhood persons receive two messages from their parents about the process of leaving. One message says, "You cannot trust yourself with choices in relation to other people; do as we say and you won't get hurt." This parental attitude communicates to the child a message of hopelessness about the freedom to choose. It tends to make cleaving a matter of human survival as children cleave to their parental world. According to the Bible, however, cleaving is oriented toward one's choices in the context of human maturity.

The other message given to children by parents is one of interpersonal trust. Children are encouraged to leave the parental nest in ways which are safe and appropriate for dependent persons. Maturing parents cheer on their offspring as they see emotional leaving taking place in their lives. They know that before their eyes they are witnessing the positive handiwork of their parenthood.

During the teen years, the process of leaving continued for Joe and Sue. Their parents did not abandon them to become totally free; this kind of abrupt leaving at the advent of the teen years usually spells disaster for emerging personalities. Neither were Joe and Sue kept under a parental umbrella we call overprotection. More and more they were trusted with decisions and responsibilities in a time of transition toward adultlike living.

As teenagers Joe and Sue met and began to date. Both were well along in the process of leaving mother and father. Because this was true, they were free to choose each other from among others whom they could have chosen. This is a point we often miss. If they had not been in a process of leaving, they would not have understood emotionally the adult meaning of leaving and cleaving. In other words, you can only cleave to your mate when you have left the world of mother and father emotionally.

As a pastoral marriage counselor, I have talked with many couples who still have the process in reverse. They are still cleaving to a world which they have never left emotionally. Because they did not leave mother and father degree by degree in childhood and adolescence, they have difficulty cleaving to their mates with adultlike freedom. Instead of cleaving to their mates, what often happens is the transferring of the old relationship pattern they had with parents to the relationship with their mates. Emotionally their mates take the place of mother and father who have not been left as the Bible commands. I have heard many marriage partners put it this way as they look at their spouses, "Why don't you grow up?" Divorce often comes from difficulty couples have in cleaving to each other physically, emotionally, and spiritually.

Sometimes, husbands and wives assist each other in the leaving process after the marriage begins. In this manner, marriages go through a process of change, where the primary allegiance moves away from the family of one's birth to the family of one's choice.

This drama of allegiance changing is symbolized beautifully in the wedding ceremony when the bride is given away. This was true for Sue and Joe. When Mr. Bennett responded to my question, "Who gives Sue to be married to Joe?" by saying, "Her mother and I do," much background communicating was happening. Joe and Sue's parents were saying something to their children on their wedding day. They were saying, "You are now free to leave our families and create your own family. We have taught you the meaning of cleaving to those you love. We have also given to you the freedom and responsibility of leaving us degree by degree. You have our blessings as you freely cleave to each other."

Sue and Joe were also addressing themselves to their parents in that moment of leave-taking. They were saying to their parents, "Thank you for assisting us to be capable of choosing a new primary person to whom we will now cleave with love, trust, and responsibility. We now leave you, not in the sense of abandonment, but in the sense of being free like you are to form a new and chosen family unit."

Their two family allegiances would continue. One would be to the family of their birth, the family which chose them and nurtured them with love and discipline toward adult maturity. The other family allegiance would be to the family of their choice. This would become the family of cleaving just as the family of their birth would be the family of leaving.

Joe and Sue left the wedding and began their marriage on that beautiful day in October. I felt good about their relationship; they were free to become one flesh in a continuing process of interpersonal communication. Their parents also felt good about their relationship. They knew that because their children had been free to leave them, they would also be free to return to them at the adult level. They were experiencing what the Bible means by "leaving and cleaving."

# 10

## Courage Is Not Loudness

### Goal
To bring the church closer to the biblical relationship between love and courage.

### Scripture
There is no fear in love, but perfect love casts out fear (1 John 4:18).

### The Church at Prayer
The worship leader can assist the gathered church to:

1. Bring their fears to the place of prayer. Covering them up with loudness or any other defense doesn't bring strength but loneliness.

2. Request that kind of love which refuses to leave the other person (spouse, child, friend, business associate, fellow church member) in relational places where fear of hurt, closeness, or rejection prevails. This, of course, is a prayer for courage as an expression of love. When we are certain that our motives are prompted by constructive and redeeming love, courage becomes stronger than fear.

Frisky arrived at our house unexpectedly one afternoon in 1943. We never learned where she came from. Someone probably left her in our yard as an unwanted puppy. When I lifted the cover of my evening paper route bag and found her snuggled there asleep, I knew she and I were meant for each other. Mom and Dad agreed! They gave their consent for the little mixed terrier to stay. "Frisky" is what we named her. She lived up to that name; her life-style was brisk and energetic.

My parents could not imagine how much having Frisky meant to me as an eight-year-old boy. I was their fourth and last child. My brother, Buddy, was three years older than I. He and his friends had a unique way of "shaking" me when I intruded too much into their peer activities. They would run by a certain cow that grazed in a nearby meadow. They knew I was afraid to get near that poker-faced animal. I would stand there and watch them disappear toward high adventure. When Frisky came, an emotional need was met in me which exists in all of us—the need to stroke another living being and to have those strokes accepted and appreciated. Frisky met that need in my emerging life. For awhile I forgot about the cow and being left by an older brother.

For about a decade, Frisky and I kept fast company. She impressed me as being a courageous little creature. Time after time I saw her set to flight birds, squirrels, and dogs larger than she. Her bark was firm and convincing. At the sign of a potential enemy she would paw the ground and send grass and earth particles flying behind her. Never once did I suspect that all of that sound and fury was a cover-up for a very insecure animal.

It all came to light one day when a cat passed through our backyard. When Frisky saw the little gray animal, she tore the air with strident, warlike sounds. The cat ac-

celerated her movement toward the east side of our
house. Frisky followed in hot pursuit; her visitor seemed
impressed with her "hot doggery." Suddenly the cat
stopped resolutely, arched her back, and fizzed at Frisky
as if to say, "OK, if you want to fight, I'm ready." Frisky
put on brakes and slid several feet through the clover.
Then she began to retreat with her barking more aggres-
sive than usual. Since Frisky did not have a rearview mirror, she did not see a small dogwood tree standing in her
path of retreat. When Frisky's hindquarters struck the
tree, I'm sure she must have thought the enemy had surrounded her. Suddenly her belligerent bark became a
pitiful cry. Poor Frisky; her ferocious offense was really a
defense behind which she had been hiding a sensitive and
frightened spirit. I still loved her after that episode, perhaps even more, for I had seen the real Frisky beneath all
of that loudness.

Years later, after reflecting on what happened to Frisky,
it occurred to me that people behave that way, too. In
fact, all of us do at times. We hide our fears behind loudness which appears to be courage. And, like Frisky, we get
louder when life has us in retreat.

I remember a woman in a previous pastorate whose
apparent courage kept her from getting close to other
people. When I became pastor of that church I was told,
"Watch out for Mrs. Jones, she'll give you plenty of trouble." When I got to know her, I understood the warnings.
She came on like a summer storm in conversation. Quite
frankly I had no desire to engage her in conversational
combat. I wanted to be her pastor but not as a target for
her hostility.

One day it happened, however. Our church secretary
buzzed me on the intercom and said, "Mrs. Jones is here
to see you." A feeling of uncontrollable dread possessed

me as I responded, "Send her in." When she entered my office, she didn't bother to sit down. Her attack began from the standing position. "How could you let the voting go the way it did in our last church business meeting?" She was referring to a certain decision made by the church. Her vote on the issue had been cast with a small minority. It was obvious that she was not happy about the decision of the church. I weighed her words, "How could you let the voting go the way it did?" She had put me in a defensive position and I wanted to defend myself. The church had voted freely without pressure from anyone. I had not let anything happen. The church had let it happen.

In that moment I felt anger churning in the pit of my stomach. I wanted to stand up and attack her just as loudly as she had attacked me. If I had done that, however, my loudness and her loudness would have been an energetic, but defeating, conversation. My loudness may have overcome hers; or, most likely, hers would have defeated mine. That would have been a winner-loser conclusion. I had counseled with too many people to want that for Mrs. Jones and myself. The winner-loser conclusion to interpersonal strain brings defeat to everybody. It is not a sign of courage in anyone.

As I sat looking up at Mrs. Jones, I made a decision that I would be her pastor, not her target. This helped me to own my anger instead of being owned by it. I said to her in an even voice, "Mrs. Jones, is something bothering you that I can help you with?" The fact that I didn't reject her surprised her. I believe she expected me to get loud with her. After all, a loud relationship is better than none at all. She sat down across from me and began to cry. Then she poured her heart out about the death of her husband, who had been dead for three years. She said, "Pastor, I've been so lonely since he died; life is just not the same when you live in a house by yourself."

What Mrs. Jones had been doing was obvious now. She had made sure that she would not receive what she really needed and wanted. She wanted closeness with other people. But she related in such a loud, rejecting manner that people either rejected her or retreated before her apparent courage. In my office that day, Mrs. Jones and I had a breakthrough. We experienced the courage which overcomes the barrier of fear, the fear of closeness. As 1 John 4:18 puts it, "Perfect love casteth out fear" (KJV). It was this spirit of Christ's love which had given us courage without loudness.

# 11

## Vision in the Night

### Goal
To rekindle in the church the gift of dreaming dreams which can be tested to see if they are visions from God.

### Scripture
And God spoke to Israel in visions of the night (Gen. 46:2).

### The Church at Prayer
The worship leader can:

1. Guide the church to a new awareness of vision as divine communication from God to His people. Praying for vision can produce spiritual openness necessary to divine revelation.

2. Call the church to a renewed emphasis on listening to God. This requires a willingness to be what Thomas Merton refers to as "The Church of the Desert." A praying church needs to pull away from a rapidly changing world in order to see God in stillness and quietness. From the desert, the church can reemerge with fresh vision for its enduring vocation of servanthood.

The people of her community called her Aunt Lindy. She was a mild-natured woman who married John Sluder before the turn of the century. They lived on ten acres of farm land in the mountains west of Asheville, North Carolina. John and Lindy were devoted to their children and lived a quiet and decent life among friends and relatives. Their lives were not given to crusades and controversy; they were content to care for their children and crops, and obey the rhythm and rituals of the passing seasons. That is, until one night when Lindy had a dream. To her it was more than a dream; it was a vision. My father, a grandson of John and Lindy Sluder, told me about the dream.

It happened about three o'clock one morning. In the dream Lindy saw a church building standing on a hill overlooking a valley. She identified the hill readily; it belonged to their land estate. The dream was quite vivid and left Lindy with warm feelings bordering on ecstasy. She aroused John and shared the dream with him. At 3:00 AM he was not a very good listener. Lindy wanted to talk about donating the land in order to build the church she had seen in her dream. John was interested in obtaining enough rest for the next day's chores. They agreed to talk about the matter again in the morning.

With the coming of dawn, Lindy was ready to talk. The smell of breakfast cooking on the wood stove provided Lindy with an appropriate background for serious conversation. "The dream was so real, John; I believe God wants us to give that land so we can have a place to worship Him," she said. John's reply was slow in coming. But when it came, it was the kind of support Lindy believed John would give. His support was qualified, however, with some practical wisdom. "Lindy," he said, "we'll give the land for a church, but before it can be built, other people are going to have to share your vision." "I know, John," she answered, "but we don't have a church building in our community and I know they'll want to accept the land and build."

John's words, "Other people are going to have to share your vision," are so true. Before a dream can become a collective blessing, we have to share it with others. That, of course, is the risk faith is willing to take. Many dreams have been born in the human spirit and have never reached the maturity of being realized because the dreamer fails to share the dream with others. The dream continues to be a spiritual infant with unrealized potential. Some dreams are shared only to be rejected or unheeded. That should not keep us from sharing our dreams. Some dreams may not be visions. The nature of a vision is its ability to bless human life if realized in a community setting.

In the Bible God gave visions to His people which were to bless human life. For example, in Genesis 46:1-4, we read that God gave Jacob a vision of the night concerning his sojourn in Egypt. The vision spoke of future blessings. In Acts 10:9-16 we read about a day vision which Simon Peter had. His vision spoke of the unprejudiced nature of God's love which is to be the church's kind of love. Both Jacob and Peter were willing to test their dreams to see if they were visions; they shared them with others who accepted their dreams as visions. The end result was divine blessing in a community setting.

Care must be taken in the process of sharing our dreams, however. Quite often the first stage of the realization of a dream which is a true vision is resistance. Only God knows the number of visions which have failed because human resistance was interpreted by the dreamer as proof that the dream was only a dream and not a vision.

This could have happened to Lindy's dream. Once she and John had agreed to give the land, she began to share her dream with the people of the community. To them, however, she had had an interesting dream. To be sure, Lindy was disappointed; she even became discouraged. But she did not abandon her dream. She believed it and kept it alive in her own spirit.

That winter brought its usual misery to the mountains of western North Carolina. Snow and howling winds came at the appointed time. With them came much illness. John and Lindy remained healthy, but their four-year-old daughter, Helen, became critically ill with pneumonia. Her parents did everything possible to keep her alive. The illness, however, was too much for Helen's weak body. She died before the coming of spring.

Friends and relatives came to support John and Lindy in their grief. Their care was accepted and appreciated. In the midst of grief bearing and sharing, someone asked the question, "Where will you bury Helen's body?" John looked at Lindy as if to say, "You answer for us." Lindy spoke from a broken and yet ready heart. "We'll bury her on the hill where the new church building is going to be." Her grief had not diminished her belief in the vision.

With snow still on the ground, the community followed John and Lindy to that windswept hill where they buried Helen's body amid the solitude and silence of the watching mountains. That day, the community accepted Lindy's dream as vision. When spring came, along with planting crops, they began to build a church building on the hill beside Helen's grave.

The church is still there, overlooking the valley. It welcomes newcomers who increasingly settle there as Asheville experiences a population explosion. Inside the church building, there still remains a rocking chair used by Aunt Lindy during the years of her decline toward death. The chair is a reminder that dreams can be visions. To Lindy, her dream was a vision in the night which became a community blessing.

# 12

# The Gift of Understanding

### Goal
To expand the meaning of Christian understanding beyond feeling to include the human faculty of judgment.

### Scripture
Keep your heart with all vigilance: for from it flow the springs of life (Prov. 4:23).

### The Church at Prayer
The worship leader can:

1. Lead the church to pray for growth in the ability to understand with judgment. This can help our understanding to avoid being gullible in the face of what often seems to be the truth about persons.

2. Pray with the church for a greater capacity to listen to others (mates, children, etc.). To truly listen to someone evokes in him or her a feeling of being understood. Such a feeling contributes to self-esteem.

All of us have what I choose to call a feeling center within us. At times we fail to recognize its presence in our inner territory. We know we have a blood circulation center (the heart), a breathing center (the lungs), and a nerve center (the brain). A cohesive center within, however, from which we experience life with feeling sensitivity often operates without our full recognition and awareness. The Bible recognizes this faith-feeling center when it instructs, "Keep your heart with all vigilance; for from it flow the springs of life" (Prov. 4:23).

At this feeling center every person experiences deep longings. One of these, which has about it a universal character, is the longing to be understood. "If only someone understood me. Nobody understands me. I am misunderstood." These are expressions heard every day. They originate from feeling centers deep within people like you and me.

This universal longing seeks for the gift of understanding which also originates deep within persons in their feeling centers. This gift of being an understanding person rests upon a refusal. The refusal has to do with judgment. The giver of understanding refuses to judge others solely on the basis of outer behavior and actions. This is true for two reasons.

First, judging others on the basis of outer behavior and actions can lead us to mistake evil for goodness. This was part of the judgment made by Adam and Eve in the Garden of Eden. To them, at least for awhile, evil appeared to be goodness. They saw only the outer nature of the serpent and his suggestion. Deception has a way of revealing only its surface identity. Lurking within, however, are the hidden agendas which spell trouble for the naive and gullible.

This was true for a bright-eyed brunette of eighteen. At

that crucial age, Cathy came to me one day and said, "Mr. Hawkins, I have met a great young man from California, and we want to get married." It all seemed so sudden to me. When they came to see me for premarital counseling, my feeling center had difficulty relating to David. He wasn't repulsive in any way; he was just too smooth to be real. My gut-level feeling was, "He's either got it all together or hiding something." My latter hunch proved to be true.

He and Cathy were married in spite of my counsel to wait awhile. About a month later they vanished from our community. Her mother told me they had gone to California. Two months later, Cathy walked into my office. She was thin and pale. The story which she told me about her trip to California was hair-raising. David was hooked on hard drugs and manipulated her into heroin use. She cried as she told me about stealing food in several states while traveling west. When they arrived in California, Cathy discovered that David had a wife in San Francisco. His parents would not allow him to enter their house. When she told David she could not live under those conditions, he threatened to kill her. In desperation she called her father who wired her enough money to return home.

Cathy had understood David the hard way. At first she had judged him only by his outside behavior and actions. That had appeared good. Within, however, at his feeling center, there dwelled a manipulative spirit with a hidden agenda. What appeared to be goodness turned out to be evil.

Second, judging persons solely on the basis of outer behavior and actions can lead us to mistake goodness for evil. For example, one day a four-year-old girl was playing in her backyard. Sue was at that young, impressionable age when human experiences are discoveries with both pleasant and unpleasant results. In her play she reached out and grabbed the knob of the water faucet. It was a brand new experience for Sue. What should have been a pleasant discovery, however, became a human nightmare. She was startled by a big black dog which suddenly passed through the yard. In her impressionable mind she made a false association. She connected turning water on with the appearance of the dog. The experience created in her an intense fear of turning on water. Weeks later, Sue and her father were in the backyard. Mr. Clark was working in the garden and called to Sue, "Sweetheart, will you turn on the water for daddy?" He wanted to water the growing vegetables. "No, I won't," came Sue's reply. Mr. Clark repeated his request only to see his daughter run into the house crying and screaming. His first thought was, "Wow, what stubbornness!" A more settled thought, however, came from his feeling center. "That's not the way Sue feels toward me," he said to himself. "Something has happened."

A moment later he sat by his daughter's side and said, "Sue, you cried when I asked you to turn on the water. Is there something about that which scares you?" In her four-year-old manner she told her daddy about the dog. In the light of what had happened, Mr. Clark understood Sue's behavior. She was not being evil or bad. She was scared and needed someone to help her overcome her fear. Moments later, Daddy and daughter stood by the outside faucet. Mr. Clark turned it on. Sue looked for the dog which did not appear. "Let's turn it on together," Mr. Clark suggested. Both hands touched the knob. Together they turned the water on and off several times. Finally Sue soloed at the faucet while laughter replaced fear on her face. Why? Because someone refused to judge her solely by her outer behavior and actions. Her dad saw beneath her negative actions and would only judge her as he touched her feeling center from his own.

Isn't this the meaning of Christ's coming to earth? He refused to judge or condemn us from a distance. He came to touch us within with the gift of understanding.

To some, that gift will be healing light. To others, it will be hurting light. His motive, however, is to help all who will open up to the penetrating light of His accurate and compassionate understanding.

# 13

# Repentance in the Church

### Goal
To revisit the church with repentance as a necessary and ongoing process in creative Christian living.

### Scripture
From that time Jesus began to preach, saying, "Repent, for the kingdom of heaven is at hand" (Matt. 4:17).

### The Church at Prayer
The worship leader can:

1. Call the church to repentance as a daily willingness to live under God's forgiving and transforming power. Prayer should be made for a willingness to bring one's life before the light of self-examination, guided by God's constructive judgments.

2. Lead the church to pray for the power to be a repentance-experiencing fellowship as a part of proclaiming the good news of the kingdom.

In announcing the coming of God's kingdom, Jesus was bringing to human relationships both the forgiveness and the judgment of God; it was His plan that both be seen as unified in the character of God and His kingdom. The mistake we tend to make in the church, however, is in separating God's forgiveness and His judgment as though one were at odds with the other. This tends to produce an attitudinal split which militates against change and growth. Attitudinal energies needed for change and growth are divided between an accepting God and a judging God.

The good news announced by Jesus is that God has come in His forgiveness and judgment for one purpose— that persons be free to move in an unending process of growth toward spiritual fulfillment and usefulness. On various occasions He revealed this truth as He spoke of the intention of His coming. "I came that they may have life, and have it abundantly" (John 10:10). "For God sent the Son into the world, not to condemn the world, but that the world might be saved through him" (John 3:17).

It is crucial then to repentance as a process of durable growth that we experience God's forgiveness and judgment in unity. For if we experience God only in terms of His judgment, we are apt to know Him attitudinally as a condemning person. In this case, religion tends to be bondage instead of freedom. On the other hand, if we experience God only in terms of forgiveness, then religion can become a spiritual nursery where we receive care, but where growth is thwarted by a sentimental view of God, which presents forgiveness without challenge toward growth.

In His presentation of the kingdom of God, Jesus brought God's forgiveness and judgment to the human situation as good news. When we see God's judgment as being inseparably related to His forgiveness, it tends to change our attitude toward His judgment. It ceases to be condemnation and becomes healing light which draws us with our hurts, pains, and sins to His forgiveness. In this sense we learn to trust God's judgment and see in it the possibility of change. This can be liberating; it cannot be forced on persons, however, who want distance from God because of their fear of being condemned. The perfect love which embraces God's forgiveness and judgment, and which is mentioned in 1 John 4:18 as having the power to banish fear, is also patient. It will not force God's judgment as healing light upon one who chooses to remain in the darkness of fear and unbelief.

Repentance involves a durable attitudinal change toward God, where one begins to see God as friend Who wills growth toward fulfillment and usefulness. It is also a durable attitudinal change toward oneself and others. At this point we need to be careful not to overclassify repentance; the attitudinal change we experience toward God is not to be viewed in isolation. It becomes relational in that it also stimulates change in the attitude we have toward ourselves and others. That is, we begin to take on toward ourselves and others the attitude which we believe God has toward us and others.

Let me illustrate. Several years ago, in my role as chaplain to parents of mentally retarded children, I counseled with a couple who had a two-year-old Downs Syndrome son. For the first fifteen minutes of our initial session, they shared with me their positive feelings about their son. They appeared to be tense. At that point I said to them, "I appreciate your sharing with me your positive feelings about your child. I do not know if you have negative feelings or not. If you do, I believe God accepts them as well as your positive ones."

At that point the counseling session became what Wayne E. Oates calls "spiritual conversation."[1] They became free to share their feelings of hurt and grief about having a mentally retarded child. Their grief did not go away. But they seemed to get the liberating message that God understood their negative feelings and did not condemn them for having them. There occurred an attitudinal change toward God, hopefully a durable one, which caused them to be freer in their attitude toward themselves and toward their two-year-old son.

The process of freedom to change would not cause their son to cease being ill; it could change the quality of their relationship so that realistic growth might occur for the parents and the child according to each one's potentialities.

A question which I want to raise now has to do with repentance and the church. The question is this: How can the church become a repentance-evoking agent in the community? I want to suggest an answer by moving away from being a repentance-demanding agent toward being a repentance-experiencing community.

To demand repentance suggests that the one demanding stands under God's judgment as condemnation. Therefore, one demands that others stand with him in his lonely spiritual territory which evokes a pittance of growth. When the church is being the church, it evokes repentance from others not by force but by incarnating repentance in its community life as supporter of durable growth. Let me illustrate.

A woman in her early twenties attended a Sunday School meeting. That Sunday morning she needed encouragement and support. She had made some unfortunate choices which had brought her much pain and anxiety.

That morning the women of the class became a repentance-experiencing community. Risking themselves, they shared data about dimensions of their personal selves where they wanted to grow. They were not seeking sentimental forgiveness from the class members and from God. They wanted help enough to bring their hurts before the judgment and forgiveness of a community of persons whom they trusted; to be sure God was at work in that context.

The visitor said nothing. The following Sunday, however, she returned and listened again. Several class members reported progress and growth with their problems. They spoke of their growth in terms of being freer in their relations with God and others, especially family members. That morning, in that context where the church was experiencing repentance in an environment of trust and openness, the young woman ceased to feel like an outsider. She risked herself by sharing her pain. The class heard her without condemning her. They simply accepted her into their quest for growth through a process of durable attitudinal change. This occurred in the presence of God's forgiveness and judgment incarnated by the church in a small group setting.

The young woman had seen a practical demonstration of repentance. In that setting, at least temporarily, love in quest of wholeness had cast out her fear of change. She experienced the church as a repentance-experiencing community.

---

1. Wayne E. Oates, *Protestant Pastoral Counseling* (Philadelphia: Westminster Press, 1962), p. 163.

# 14

# Forgiveness Is Not Easy

### Goal

To clarify the interpersonal nature of forgiveness. Between God and us, relationships are more important than what breaks them. The fact that God sent the forgiving Christ to reconcile us makes this truth very clear. This is to be true between us and others.

### Scripture

Then Peter came up and said to him, "Lord, how often shall my brother sin against me, and I forgive him? As many as seven times?" Jesus said to him, "I do not say to you seven times, but seventy times seven" (Matt. 18: 21-22).

### The Church at Prayer

The worship leader can:

1. Call the church to experience God's forgiveness as a freeing reality in the present. God is willing to remove the heavy debt of guilt. Prayer can bring us into His forgiving presence.

2. Make the church aware of self-forgiveness. All of us have a relationship with ourselves. Often forgiveness is kept from the self by the self. If God forgives us, we need to let His grace come in as the basis of our own self-forgiveness.

3. Bring the gathered church to a forgiving attitude toward areas of human living where reconciliation is

needed. As God values His relationship with us as being more important than that which breaks it, so must we. Otherwise, we shut off the continuing flow of His forgiveness toward us.

Forgiveness was not easy for me as a nine-year-old boy. Back then every Friday was payday at our house. It was payday for Dad, and, also, payday for my brother, Buddy, and me. As soon as Dad came home from the textile plant where he worked, he would give us a nickel each for foolish candy money. One Friday, with nickels in hand, we were running toward Dabney's store to buy candy. Suddenly my nickel fell from my hand and began to roll down the street. Before I could reach it, a teenager grabbed it. He said to me, "Finders, keepers; losers, weepers." I wept all right, but he walked away with my nickel. In that moment I didn't want to forgive that rascal. He didn't want my forgiveness; he wanted my nickel. If he and I were to meet today, chances are we could laugh about what happened that day. But then it hurt me deeply.

Jesus never said that forgiveness is easy. He simply spoke of it as a liberating experience which blesses the quality of interpersonal relationships. One of His parables illustrates this beautifully. The setting for the parable was a question which Simon Peter asked about forgiveness. He wanted to know how many times one should forgive his brother. Before Jesus could give the answer, Simon impulsively stated what he thought was reasonable.

Outdoing the rabbis of the times who admonished the sufficiency of three forgiving times toward a brother, Peter doubled that number and added an additional time for good measure. He suggested seven times as an appropriate forgiveness countdown. Jesus used Peter's openness as an occasion to teach a remarkable lesson about the dynamics of forgiveness. After taking Peter's mathematics of seven times and expanding it beyond an exercise in bookkeeping, He presents a parable in which forgiveness is seen as an attitude experienced at the feeling center of one's being (Matt. 28:21-35).

In the parable, a king decides to settle accounts with his servants. One servant is brought to him who owes an enormous amount of money. The amount is set at ten thousand talents, each talent being equivalent to about a thousand dollars. This may have been Jesus' way of illustrating the impossibility of human effort to produce divine forgiveness. At any rate, there was no way for the servant to balance up with the king. The servant is at the point of being sold with his wife, children, and possessions because of the debt which defies payment.

What a vivid picture of the human plight of alienating guilt carried before God! The servant as an act of self-preservation falls on his knees and implores the king's patience until he is able to pay everything. Payment, of course, was not possible. The king, however, out of pity releases him through forgiveness. The debt is deleted from the king's ledger. The servant walks out having been offered forgiveness. It is quite evident, however, that he had not received the king's offer as forgiveness.

This is the penetrating truth which the parable gives about the nature of forgiveness. Once on the outside the servant sees another servant who owes him about twenty dollars. If he had received what the king had given him as forgiveness, his attitude toward that fellow human being would have been a forgiving one. He would have said something like this: "The most wonderful thing has just happened to me. I owed the king an unpayable debt and he set me free from that burdensome load. Therefore, I want to set you free. I want to forgive you as the king forgave me." Instead, he demanded the twenty dollars from his fellow servant and had him thrown into prison when payment could not be made.

We wonder what might have been in the mind of the first servant when he left the king's presence. Perhaps he thought, *Well, I am glad the king has finally realized how much I do for him. It is no wonder he released me from the debt.* On the other hand, he may have suffered from such low self-esteem that he could not trust the king's offer. Whatever his thoughts may have been, one fact is sure. He did not receive what the king offered. The king forgave him, but he was not forgiven. The attitude of forgiveness would have caused him to breath the fresh air of freedom, joy, and peace. His latter condition, however, was worse than the first. He was placed in prison for the unforgiving deed committed toward a fellow servant.

We must be careful at this point. If not, we shall hear Jesus saying in this parable, "You must forgive others; if not, God the King will not forgive you." This can reinforce our guilt by our faking forgiveness toward others in order to win forgiveness from a stingy God. That is not what Jesus is saying at all. The parable teaches us that forgiveness once received as a *freeing* gift, sets us free to give forgiveness as a *relational* gift.

The way we know we are living in God's forgiveness is by the growth of a forgiving spirit in our human relationships. In other words, we become freer to grow through forgiveness toward self-fulfillment and self-giving. This becomes a matter of how we see God seeing us, how we see ourselves, and how we see others. The poor servant never saw the king seeing him as a forgiving person. He passed on to his fellow servant the same attitude he felt coming from the king and the same attitude he had toward himself.

Forgiveness becomes real when a new attitude of acceptance on our part is able to trust the durable reliability of acceptance on God's part. This attitude, in turn, becomes a relational gift with which we are blessed and through which we bless others. Often one's family becomes the blessed recipient of forgiveness as the freedom to grow. Let me illustrate.

A minister returned home after a busy day of pastoral duties. He greeted his wife and six-year-old daughter, June, and then hurried upstairs to pack a suitcase for an overnight trip. June followed her dad upstairs, a natural move for a daughter devoted to her father. Richard was busy putting items into the suitcase when June fell against the bed with her body. The suitcase and its contents fell to the floor. Richard said he spoke very harshly to June. She had become the victim of frustrations which had been stored up for days. With her heart wounded, she went downstairs.

Richard quickly finished packing and joined his family at the table. When he was ready to leave, he kissed his wife, Joan, and then asked June, "Are you going to kiss Daddy good-bye?" Her nonverbal head shake communicated a firm negative. Richard put his suitcase down and descended to her level and said, "June, I know I hurt you when I spoke to you upstairs. I'm sorry. But you could have been more careful with Daddy's suitcase, too. Now, why don't we forgive each other?" Richard said she fell into his arms with a smile; they parted with their relationship blessed by restored communication.

June was learning that she was a living center from whom the spirit of forgiveness could flow toward others. Moreover, there was growing in her the capacity to both give and receive forgiveness as a relational gift. To be sure, she made the association between her father and God, the Father.

# 15

# Thoughts on Freedom

### Goal
To bring realistic insights to the meaning of human freedom. Some seem to view freedom as getting away from themselves. True freedom brings us to ourselves, and to the God Who made us.

### Scripture
If you continue in my word, you are truly my disciples, and you will know the truth, and the truth shall make you free (John 8:31-32).

### The Church at Prayer
The worship leader can:

1. Call the church to the truth in prayer. Jesus says knowing the truth is related to being set free. Surely He had in mind truth about God, self-truth, and truth about life in general. True praying does not lead us away from truth but in it and toward it.

2. Lead the church to confess areas of life where bondage needs to give way to freedom. Jesus calls us to abide in His Word. In praying for freedom we must dwell in His Spirit and Word.

Recently I talked with a group of college students about the meaning of human freedom. In our conversation they expressed to me their frustration about what they called, "life without freedom." One student said, "We were not free to choose the period of history in which our lives would be lived." Another said, "We were not free to choose our parents and family." Other areas of nonfreedom mentioned were physical characteristics, nationality, and sexuality.

They were right. We are not free to choose the time, place, conditions, gender, and persons related to our birth. These dimensions of selfhood are given to us. What does it mean, then, to be free as a person?

Personal freedom has its beginnings in our acceptance of the nature of what has been given to us. There are persons who resist for a lifetime what has been given to them by birth and family identification. Instead of accepting the fact that they are not free to be other persons, they seek to escape from the persons they are. In doing so they deny their past. They give themselves a message which says, "We're really not who we are."

To deny our past, however, is to reject not only our birth and family identification, it is to reject ourselves in the process. We are the products of our past; whatever was given to us belongs to the personal history which is ours. We may attempt to deny it. When we do, our past becomes a prison which enslaves us. For, in attempting to deny our past we hide the roots, the only roots which can express themselves in real personhood. Freedom comes when we accept the roots of birth, parents, and family as ours; we cannot trade our roots in and get a new set.

If we had been free to choose the nature of our birth and family identification, perhaps we would have chosen differently. That kind of freedom does not exist for us humans, however. We are free to take what has been given to us and either reject it or accept it. Accepting it is not only the beginning of freedom, it is the beginning of maturity.

Human freedom is also related to choosing. People the world over have learned a fundamental lesson about human life; persons grow through choosing. To choose not to choose is to deny one's right and responsibility to be free. To keep another person from making his own choices as he grows biologically is to damage his growth toward maturity as a person. No one can be free without choosing.

The beauty of our right to choose can be seen in the fundamental difference between nature and human nature. This truth came to me during my twentieth summer. I had just finished my junior year at Furman University and had gone to assume my duties as minister to youth at the Tabernacle Baptist Church in Union, South Carolina.

As a part of my orientation to Union and its surroundings, the youth of the church insisted on my seeing White Lake. Even though it was miles from their community, they considered it to be one of the sights to see. They said to me, "Just wait until you see it; it's beautiful." When I saw it, I agreed. It was a place of enchanting natural beauty. I drove to the lake just after nightfall one evening. All of the ingredients seemed to be present for a "time to remember."

From the pier where I sat, I was engulfed by a scene which is still a memory treasure tucked away in my mind. The lake was surrounded by graceful Carolina pines. They· stood guard, giving the lake a sense of boundary and security. On the tops of several pines a summer moon, showing its full face, cradled itself, and sent beams of light dancing across the lake to the pier where I sat. The scene was mellowed by a subdued breeze which pushed its way gently through the pines.

In that hour of communion with nature and with God, I expressed gratitude for nature's beauty and my capacity to celebrate it. And yet, in the midst of that blessing the thought occurred to me, *This is beautiful because it has to be that way.* Nature cannot choose its beauty; it has to be beautiful. The moon cannot refuse to shine; it has no choice in the matter. The water cannot refuse to reflect the moonbeams and the pine trees cannot stop whispering the wind's voice. All of this is mechanical; nature shares its beauty without thinking, feeling, and choosing.

I left White Lake with an appreciation for the beauty I had seen there. My deeper appreciation, however, was reserved for the beauty which comes from people who are free to choose patterns of beauty and to appreciate that beauty within themselves and others. The Creator could have given us beauty without freedom. If that had been the case, He would have placed us with the trees, wind, water, and other component parts of a beautiful but impersonal creation. It is in choosing, that we discover the secrets of our human freedom. In being free to choose, we become persons. In being responsible to God, ourselves, and others in our choosing, we reflect the glory of the Creator. That's real beauty.

# 16

# Who Is Jesus in Relation to Power?

### Goal
To get in touch with power sources in nature and people and to see their limit in comparison with Christ's power.

### Scripture
And they were afraid, and they marveled, saying to one another, "Who then is this, that he commands even wind and water, and they obey him?" (Luke 8:25).

### The Church at Prayer
The worship leader can:

1. Bring the church to an awareness that all created power has limits. That means our powers have limits; so do the powers of others. This is not a put-down; it's just reality. In accepting our powers we need to see in them both potential and boundary.

2. Call the church to faith in terms of interdependence. Christ is with us and augments our powers with His eternal power. More than that, He transforms us with His power of love. Faith can release His power in us and between us.

There has streaked across our personal, national, and international skies a staggering comet called the power crisis. The crisis has at least three dimensions. The dimensions are nature, government, and people.

The power crisis in nature centers in the question, "Can we get in touch with nature's limitations to sustain and support human life?" We depend on nature for air, water, and vegetation. And yet, more and more we wound nature. We contaminate our air and water supply and threaten the balance which exists as a mutual support system between the plant and animal kingdoms.

With such abuse inflicted upon the component parts of nature, one wonders if nature will finally be forced to communicate the message, "OK, it's enough. I can no longer sustain you. You have wounded me fatally, and in return I can only give you death. For in my demise your death comes, also."

If we cannot get in touch with nature's limitations to sustain our kind, we may, because of our inability to respect the integrity and value of nature, join the dinosaurs as creatures incapable of environmental adaptation. This is a somber thought. And yet, ecological concern is a concern about the power crisis in nature.

Just as the crisis in nature is not the "energy crunch," the crisis in government is not the still-remembered Watergate affair. The lamentable crisis in government lies, I think, exactly where it does in nature. "Can we get in touch with the limitations of government to solve our problems? Can we develop a proper balance between expectations of what government can and ought to do for us, and our responsibility of what we can and ought to do for ourselves?" The limitations do exist. If we cannot get in touch with those limitations, government may reach a moment of truth in which it says, "OK, I can no longer fulfill your expectations; they are beyond my powers and energies."

The power crisis in people is evident in the apathy-filled conversations one hears. Adults, youth, and even children are heard saying, at times, "We're bored with things; there's nothing left for us to be or do." In many people there seems to be an inner void—an inner tear which somehow never drops. In their spiritual depths they seem to be saying, "We have powers of mind, body, and spirit, but we feel torn and fragmented. We cannot put our powers together."

Is there someone who can help us put it all together in terms of our powers? The New Testament gives an answer of hope to those who ask this question. In a sense we all ask this question as we stand in the dimension of our spiritual brokenness. The answer comes in the form of a person. Luke presents a vivid picture of Him as He stands between two power crises (Luke 8:22-39).

One is a power crisis in nature. In reality, the crisis is in the band of men who are with Jesus in the boat. The power in nature triggers the crisis. Luke says a storm arose. The sea became like a caldron of vibrating liquid; waves played havoc with the boat. The disciples were afraid; they saw in nature's power a manifestation of the demonic. They turned to Jesus. How will He meet this crisis? He could have sought to destroy the demon. Instead He spoke to the storm; He held a conversation with nature. This eternal Christ knew there was more there than the storm. Thus, He gives a command in which He rebukes the storm. In essence He commanded nature to manifest another side of its personality. The storm left and there was another face of nature in its place. Jesus did not condemn the storm; He spoke to nature with respect and out of creative dialogue with the creation, communion replaced chaos. He was not afraid of nature's stormy side. He respected nature as a being worthy of conversation and sensitive enough to respond to human need.

Oh, that we might see nature this way! She is a person to be respected and not an inanimate object to be exploited and feared. The power crisis in nature demands that we recover the conversational dimension of our relationship with nature. Jesus revealed this to us. To Him nature is to be celebrated, not controlled; to be respected as a kinswoman of our common ancestry. Our survival is related to our recognition of nature as a part of our Father's family. Jesus did!

From the crisis at sea, Jesus and His disciples move to the shores of the Gadarenes. They hear a man's voice coming from the tomb area. He has been banished from his community. People have seen him only as evil; "He has a demon," they say. The man is torn on the inside. He cannot put his powers together. What will Jesus do? Will He echo the popular condemnation of this man? Let's see.

He approached the man, looked deeply within him, and, in essence, said to him what He said to nature—"Let me see your other side, your other face!" "What is your name?" was Jesus' way of putting it. In that question He held conversation with the man who was torn and fragmented. The man wondered why Jesus would speak to him. He was demonic! He had been banished by society. They had seen him as incapable of controlling the powers within him. He had come to see himself that way, also.

Jesus saw beneath the jagged edges of this man's being controlled by outside forces. Still within him was a center of freedom where faith is possible. He spoke to that center. He addressed the person, not the demon. In other words, Jesus said, "I came from the God Who made you. There is within you the gift of personhood." As the Son of

God, Jesus spoke the creative words, "Bring forth," and out of chaos, order came to the tormented man. He spoke the redemptive words, "Come forth," and out of the inner tomb the man was resurrected to wholeness. When the people saw him they were amazed that he was "clothed and in his right mind" (v. 35). Jesus had helped him to consolidate his fragmented spirit.

We identify with this man. In our world of stress, power confusion, and failure, we become torn and fragmented. We cannot heal ourselves. This is when, into our self-made tombs, the Lord of redemption comes to ask the redemptive question, "What is your name?" With creative hope, Jesus waits for the appearing of the person clothed in his right relationship with God.

In a trust relationship, redemption comes and we find ourselves put together within, with our powers consolidated. But that's not enough! The powers which are *consolidated* must be *commissioned!* This happened to the man whom Jesus healed. After his powers were consolidated, he wanted to go with Jesus. He was ready for service out of gratitude. Jesus commissioned him to stay at home and share the good news with familiar people. He also commissions us to share our adopted name, Christian, with others.

# 17

# Is Anyone Among Us Perfect?

### Goal
To aid us to be aware at all times of our own imperfect nature and that of others.

### Scripture
Beloved, believe not every spirit, but try the spirits whether they are of God: because many false prophets are gone out into the world (1 John 4:1, KJV).

### The Church at Prayer
The worship leader can:

1. Lead the church to pray for a true spirit of humility which opens the heart and mind to God's truth revealed through the Holy Spirit.

2. Stress the importance of each person staying in touch with his or her vulnerability before evil's deception and power.

3. Call the church to trust one another and respect every person's right and responsibility to interpret the Bible and its application to life under God's guiding counsel.

What I now choose to write comes from a feeling of grief. I grieve over the confusion which exists among many Christians today. I grieve over the perplexity on the faces of fine Christian lay people. They love God and are committed to the proclamation of the good news of Jesus Christ to people. "What's wrong?" they ask. "Why is there so much misunderstanding within denominations? So many people use so many labels in so many different ways that we are not sure what to call one another.

Why do we have all the confusion? I have no final answer. I do have, however, a belief and a conviction. Here it is: We have not heard what 1 John 4:1 has to say about "trying the spirits" to see if they are of God. Recently I spoke on this subject to a Wednesday evening prayer service group in our church. In prayerfully planning my thoughts, it occurred to me that there are three ways we can try or test the spirits.

First, **we try our own spirits.** I believe this is where trying the spirits is to begin. If I give myself the right to be wrong, then I will constantly try my spirit and bring it to self-examination and other examination. If I feel my spirit, however, is above trying, then I assume for myself perfection in spiritual matters. That would mean, for example, that my interpretation of Scripture would be perfect. That is. a claim no one can rightfully make. Throughout the history of Christianity there have been too many people hurt by those who have said, "The Lord said to me," without making it clear that what they meant was—"this is my interpretation of what the Lord said."

Ministers of the gospel, I believe, have a responsibility to try their own spirits and let their congregation know that their preaching is an interpretation, an inspired one, but an interpretation nonetheless, subject to human imperfection. It's not that we want or choose to be imperfect; it's that we are. Inspiration does not eradicate human imperfection. By trying our spirits, we put ourselves under a self-discipline which can help to deliver us from confusing our spirits and their promptings with the Spirit and promptings of God. "For now we see through a glass, darkly; . . . now I know in part" (1 Cor. 13:12, KJV).

Second, **we try the spirits of others.** "But didn't Jesus say that we are not to judge others lest we be judged ourselves?" one may ask. Yes, He did. But He continued to tell us in the seventh chapter of Matthew to get rid of the problem in our own eye and then we would be able to deal with the problem in our brother's eye (v. 5). First, we try our own spirits, then, with our own continuing imperfection in mind, we can better deal with the imperfection in others. When we see others who are as imperfect as we, behaving as though they were perfect, we try that spirit and assess it for what it usually is—inflated pride. No one group or individual has a corner on this spiritual malady.

Back in the 1960s, while serving as pastor of the Old Fort Baptist Church, Old Fort, North Carolina, I read an account of a young lady who lived in the mountains. She had two boyfriends, both of whom had marital intentions toward her. One day one of them came to see her and said, "Mary, I've prayed about our relationship and God has spoken to me and said it is His will for us to get married." Mary was impressed with his earnestness. Several days later the other boyfriend came to see Mary and shared the same revelation from the Lord about Mary and him. He was just as sincere and earnest. Do you know what Mary did? She tried their spirits and decided that neither of them was of the Lord. She then married a bright young fellow from another town.

Christians have a right and responsibility to do what Mary did—try the spirits to see if they are of God. This is part of what we mean by soul competency and the priesthood of believers. No one person or group of persons can become the human channel through which the Spirit of God is obliged to convey divine truth to others. Every one of us should be willing to have his or her spirit put on trial so that human imperfection and divine perfection might be kept where they truly are—separate and, yet, interdependent.

Third, **we try the spirit of evil.** M. Scott Peck, in his book, *People of the Lie,* has brought a penetrating challenge to the contemporary church to take evil seriously.[1] Dr. Peck, a competent psychiatrist and a committed Christian, speaks of evil as being truly existent as a spiritual person. The intention of Satan, according to Peck, is to destroy life. Satan's methods are deception, disguise, and an unwillingness to be open to self-examination and examination by others. Two of the sure signs of evil in human life are the presence of confusion and an unwillingness to take responsibility for one's own evil. That is, evil is never in me; it is always in someone else or in that other group. Adam blamed his evil on Eve and Eve blamed hers on the serpent. God held each responsible for his and her own evil.

Projecting evil on another as blame is what Jesus commands us not to do. He said, "Judge not, that you be not judged" (Matt. 7:1). The Lord is not telling us not to judge evil. He is telling us where we need to begin. We need to begin with our own evil and try it in our own spirits and keep on trying it, for evil will keep on penetrating our spirits, prayers, and relationships. As we are aware of our own vulnerability to Satan's daily program of attack, then we are experientially and compassionately ready to try the spirits of others.

A part of our problem in trying evil in ourselves and

others relates to our spiritual insensitivity to evil's basic strategy. Helmut Thielicke, a German theologian and pastor, in his book, *How the World Began*, illustrates this truth. He wrote that in the 1950s he and some of his students put on a Punch-and-Judy show for refugee children from East Germany. In the show he played the part of the devil. He wielded a horrible, fiery red puppet in one hand and mustered up a menacing and horrible voice to represent all the horrible discords of hell. Then with tones brimming with sulphur he advised the children to indulge in every conceivable naughtiness: You never need to wash your feet at night; you can stick your tongue out at anybody you want to; and be sure to drop banana skins on the street so people will slip on them. The results were amazing. The children suddenly stopped sticking out their tongues and actually shouted him down with ear-splitting protests.

What made the difference? Dr. Thielicke did what Satan and evil do not do. He identified himself as the devil in the show; he was out in the open. This is not the way evil actually works. It comes in very attractive disguises, quoting Scripture, talking religion, building images of others as demons and itself as God's special protector. Then comes the confusion, division, and, finally, destructiveness. This is the way Satan is successful in churches, marriages, families, and denominational conventions. It hooks us on getting rid of itself in somebody else. Human evil does not turn on itself; it does not try its own spirit. If it did, it would put itself in the light where salvation can come as healing and cure.

Is there hope? Yes, there is, but it is not easy. Hope comes when from wherever we look on others (i.e., from a pulpit, president's chair, marriage partner's seat, parent's perspective, child's view of parents, the pew's view of the pulpit, the single's view of others), trying the spirits begins as responsible self-examination and continues as responsible spiritual examination of others. Sorting out the evil in our own spirits enables us to speak the truth in love to others. Evil is defenseless against this kind of honesty which keeps on bringing its imperfect spirit before the perfect Spirit of God for correction and care.

Even after Simon Peter made his great, divinely inspired confession of faith and heard Jesus' enthusiastic congratulations, "Thou art Peter, and upon this rock I will build my church" (Matt. 16:18, KJV), he still was a sinful and imperfect person. So were all the church leaders after him. So are you and I.

---

1. M. Scott Peck, *People of the Lie: The Hope for Healing Human Evil* (New York: Simon & Schuster Inc., 1983).

# 18

# The Various Faces of Tears

### Goal
To prepare the church to more fully participate in the rich spiritual meaning of our Lord's Supper. All of our tears, seen and unseen, are welcomed at the family table.

### Scripture
And I heard a great voice from the throne saying, "Behold, the dwelling of God is with men. He will dwell with them, and they shall be his people, and God himself will be with them; he will wipe away every tear from their eyes, and death shall be no more, neither shall there be mourning nor crying nor pain anymore, for the former things have passed away" (Rev. 21:3-5).

### The Church at Prayer
The worship leader can call the church to prayer as gratitude for a table prepared. The invitation can then be extended, "Come and share."

Join me now at our Lord's table; it will be the pulpit for our worship experience this evening. That puts all of us on the same level. I like that.

Here at the family table I want to ask you a question. When was the last time you can remember crying? Was it last week? Was it last month or last year? You may say, "Oh, but I don't cry." But you do. Someone has said there are dry tears or silent tears. You may not shed them on the face, but you do shed them on the inside. We all cry. Our Creator has given us the biological equipment for crying. All of us have tear ducts and tear canals. If you look closely you can see the little openings through which the tears come.

Have you ever noticed how people cry for different reasons? Whatever those reasons are, I believe our Lord welcomes them at the family table. The day will come, according to Revelation, when He will return and wipe our tears away. For now, however, we cry and our tears have meaning. Let's look, then, at the various faces of tears.

Some people cry when they experience joy. I have stood here in this place, not for communion, but for weddings, and have seen tears of joy. I look at the mother of the bride and sometimes she is crying. Then I say, "Who gives this woman to be married to this man?" And Daddy says, "Her mother and I . . ." and the tears come. They are tears of joy. He's not joyful about getting rid of his daughter; he is happy because of parental love being fulfilled in marital love. There is a significant place for the tears of joy at our Father's table.

There are people who cry when they laugh. If you knew the family of my birth, you would know persons who, when they laugh heartily, start crying. I don't know how God has put you together biologically and emotionally, but that's the way my family does it, especially my mother and Aunt Sally. At home we have a picture board on the wall next to the family table. In the middle of it is a picture of Pat and me as we were leaving for our honeymoon in June 1957. All around that picture are other pictures of family, friends, and shared happenings. The images of my mother and Aunt Sally are on one of those pictures. When I see it, I remember how they used to laugh. Some people, when they laugh, laugh in the nose area. Others laugh in the eyes, the nose, and the mouth. But there are people who laugh all over. Mother and Aunt Sally laughed all over. Their toes got into their laughter. Then, at a certain point in their laughing, tears would begin to flow down their faces. That's the way God put them together. There is a place for the gift of laughter at the family table. Sometimes it give us blessed release from stress and burden.

Our tears can also express a sense of wonder. I like to go out and look at the things of nature—the majestic mountains of East Tennessee and the processing in and out of the seasons. When I do this, often I get lost in a sense of wonder and find myself with tears in my eyes before I know it. I'm not ashamed of that.

The most moving experience of wonder, however, did not come from nature. It came as I stood at a hospital door looking at a young mother and her first baby. We are not supposed to go in a hospital room when mothers are with their babies. I didn't go in. I stayed at the door. Joan had her baby cradled in her arms, and I'll never forget that expression on her face and those tears in her eyes as she said, "Pastor, it's wonderful!" What she was saying was, "It's full of wonder." There's a place for that kind of wonder at the family table.

There are tears which communicate a response to pain. We know that. When we are truly sensitive to our fellow human beings, we will learn of their sufferings. Some people do their work accompanied by varying degrees of pain. Others bring pain to their intimate relationships. Some are heroes and heroines of pain. They hurt, cry, and grow spiritually in spite of it.

One form of pain is human disappointment. When my brother, Virgil, was a child, the Depression of the 1930s was full blown. One summer day somebody brought him a beautiful, luscious peach. It was his very own! Virgil rushed up to the community building where the men gathered to play dominoes and walked in with the peach in his hand. Henry Jones saw the peach, reached out and grabbed it and said, "Virgil, let me have some of that." Then he got his pocketknife and cut the peach in half and pretended to start eating it. When he looked back at Virgil, he saw that tears were rolling down his face and his mouth was quivering with disappointment. Henry said that if he could have gone out and bought a bushel of peaches for Virgil Hawkins, he would have done it. Then he returned the peach to Virgil.

Children do have disappointments. Sometimes as adults we forget how they can hurt on the inside. To those of you who are children, I want to say, God knows about your hurts. He knows every tear that falls on the inside or which comes down your face.

I attended a pastoral care conference in Louisville, Kentucky, in the spring of 1984. One of the speakers, Dr. Myron Madden, shared with us that a lady came to him for counseling and said, "Dr. Madden, I've just turned forty and I can't stop crying; what am I going to do?" He smiled at her and said, "Just think about how it's going to be when you turn fifty. When you turn fifty, you'll remember how nice it was when you turned forty." She left Dr.

Madden, happy about being forty; her tears, however, were OK.

The last face of tears which I hold up before our awareness is appreciation. I remember a lady in the First Baptist Church, Statesboro, Georgia, who shared her appreciation in a unique manner. When we moved from Statesboro in 1980 after my being the church's pastor for five years, we had the usual termination rituals. People say things at those times which are not shared as frequently in the course of ongoing relationships. During a reception the lady came up and grabbed my hand. There were tears in her eyes. My wife, Pat, and I had moved with her family through some deep waters of hurt and pain. She didn't say a single word; she just gripped my hand, and her face said it all. I'll never forget that communication of gratitude and appreciation.

We come to this table with our tears of gratitude for what the Lord has meant to us. I remember that episode when Jesus went to the home of Simon the Pharisee (Luke 7:36-50). Luke says it was mealtime and that a woman came in, approached the table and began to cry. Her tears were an expression of gratitude and love. She bathed the Master's feet with her tears and wiped them away with her hair. Simon became annoyed with the woman and registered his complaint to Jesus. Jesus turned to him and the conversation went something like this: "Simon, two people owed a creditor, one about $50 and the other about $1,000. Then the creditor came in and said, 'I'm going to forgive both of you.'" Jesus asked, "Who do you think will be the most grateful?" Simon said, "The one who was forgiven the most." Jesus said, "Now you've got it, Simon. This woman was forgiven a lot, and her gratitude and love are great." When we really get in touch with that which Jesus has done for us in forgiveness, we, too, gather at the table in gratitude.

Project with me now from this table to that time when Jesus Christ is going to return. Revelation says that when He comes, He's going to do something. He will wipe away all of our tears. Well, I want to make a confession to you. When the Lord returns, I know Frank Hawkins enough to know what I'm going to do. I'm going to have myself a good cry—a cry of gratitude for all He has done for me. Then I'll say, "OK, Master, wipe them away. I won't need them anymore." There will be no more crying, no more pain, no more death. Then He will take us into the eternal banquet and serve us and let us serve around His blessed table.

Here then is His invitation to you: Bring your tears, bring all of your emotions, bring everything you are on the inside, knowing that He accepts it and offers forgiveness for what needs forgiven, and affirmation for the good which is growing in us. Isn't this what it means to be family with Him at His table?